Guide for Investigator Initiated Trials

Gerhard Fortwengel

Guide for Investigator Initiated Trials

Isabel Böckler
Rafael Dymek
Sebastian Häckl
Alexander Hahn
Katrin Hertwig
Cynthia Kuhn
Birgit Lindner
Sarah Lütkens
Christoph Neumann
Marcus Paul
Madlen Pomp
Nadja Schachteli

KARGER

Basel · Freiburg · Paris · London · New York · New Delhi ·
Bangkok · Bejing · Tokyo · Kuala Lumpur · Singapore · Sydney

Library of Congress Cataloging-in-Publication Data

Fortwengel, Gerhard.
  Guide for investigator initiated trials / Gerhard Fortwengel.
        p. ; cm.
  Includes bibliographical references and index.
  ISBN 978-3-8055-9684-8 (spiral bound soft cover : alk. paper) -- ISBN
978-3-8055-9685-5 (e-ISBN)
  1. Clinical trials. I. Title.
  [DNLM: 1. Clinical Trials as Topic. 2. Research Design. W 20.5]
  R853.C55F672 2011
  615.5072′4--dc22
                                                    2010053999

© Copyright 2011 by S. Karger AG
P.O. Box, CH-4009 Basel (Switzerland)
Printed in Switzerland on acid-free and non-aging paper (ISO 9706) by Reinhardt Druck, Basel
www.karger.com
ISBN 978–3–8055–9684–8
e-ISBN 978–3–8055–9685–5

Contents

Example documents, in Word or PDF format, are available to download via the Karger website. Please visit: www.karger.com/giit

Risk-Benefit Analysis

A risk-benefit analysis for a clinical trial is provisionally based on the preclinical phase of the medicinal product. The sponsor-investigator team needs to evaluate the toxicological tests and results as well as submit the data to the competent health authorities, with a projection of all the possible risks for the proposed trial subjects.

This provisional projection, however, cannot provide a reliable statement to the 'true' risk-benefit assessment of an investigational medicinal product (IMP).

Regulatory Reference

!   International Conference on Harmonization and Good Clinical Practice (ICH GCP) Guideline, Chapters 2.2, 3.1.4, 3.3.8 (b), 4.8.10 (i), 4.10.2, 5.19.3 (b), 6.2.3, 7.1, 7.3.6 (b)
!   Declaration of Helsinki
!   EU Directive 2001/20/EC, Art. 1 (2), (18), Art. 4, Art. 5

Responsibilities

The sponsor-investigator team must collect all available information to be able to undertake an adequate risk-benefit analysis. Usually, the Investigator's Brochure (IB) and/or the Summary of Product Characteristics (SmPC) – the latter available when the medicinal product planned to be further investigated is already on the market – are the main documents for which the sponsor-investigator should request the medicinal product manufacturer to provide.

More often is the case when the sponsor-investigator has no prior clinical data to accomplish a true risk-benefit analysis. Thus, this analysis is an evaluation of the available knowledge. The important clinical data will be gathered during the trial.

There may be other available information sources: sponsor-investigators should check the supplemental information in the SmPC and ask the manufacturer of the medicinal product if there are any prior risk-benefit analyses.

see 11
Investigator's Brochure/Summary of Product Characteristics

One of the most important concepts in a clinical trial is to ensure and protect the well-being of the involved trial subjects. Therefore, at all times, you must act to minimize the risk to human beings, regardless of the trial performance.

During the entire study, the data needs to be reviewed and evaluated routinely. Usually, a team of experts (or a formal Data Monitoring Committee [DMC]) review the data and decide on a periodic basis, whether the study should continue as planned.

Regulatory Reference

! ICH GCP Guideline, Chapters 2.2, 3.1.4, 3.3.8 (b), 4.8.10 (i), 4.10.2, 5.19.3 (b), 6.2.3, 7.1, 7.3.6 (b)
! Declaration of Helsinki
! EU Directive 2001/20/EC, Art. 1 (2), (18), Art. 4, Art. 5

Responsibilities

Definition

The risk-benefit-analysis describes, on the one hand, the proportion of the potential treatment efficacy, and on the other hand, the proportion of all the possible types of risks to the study patient – whether due to the quality, safety or efficacy of the investigational product. This proportion is crucial for the approval.

Importance

To obtain a meaningful risk-benefit analysis, there are two important considerations. Not only is the most favourable benefit of the investigational product for the trial subject of importance, but also the cognition of potential risks of therapy.

There are some diseases (e.g. cancer, cardiac infarction) that have a very high mortality. In this instance, it might be beneficial to take a higher risk with the therapy. For diseases that are symptomatic but do not jeopardize the overall health of the patient (e.g. common cold), it has to be ensured that the risk is considerably less than the benefit. In the figure, the ideal ratio would be in the lower right-hand corner, i.e. the benefits of treatment outweigh the risks.

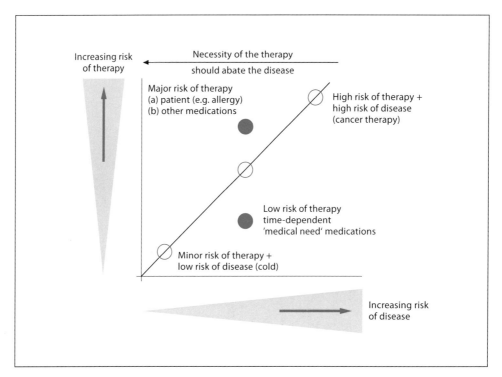

Deliberations in Risk-Benefit Analysis of Pharmacotherapy.

The ICH GCP assumes that the risk-benefit ratio is of prime importance for each trial subject as well as for the public health. However, an official criterion for the ratio calculation does not exist. It always is an individual decision how to make this analysis or calculation. At the time of the approval, it is sufficient that the evaluation of this ratio is provisional.

Responsibilities in Each Study Phase

a Phase I:

The sponsor-investigator, the regulatory health authorities and an Independent Ethics Committee (IEC) are competent to estimate the ratio between risk and benefit by reference to the data recording safety and effectiveness.

b Phase II/III:

The sponsor-investigator has to inform the health authority and the IEC about sudden unexpected serious adverse reactions (SUSARs). Furthermore, the sponsor-investigator must supply a safety report annually. Based on those documents, the health authority and the IEC have to decide if the risk-benefit ratio is acceptable to continue the trial.

see 19
Pharmacovigilance

Advice – Hints and Tips

- The risks and the benefits have to be reviewed and discussed by the sponsor-investigator team. The data included in the review should be balanced for the planned trial. Ideally, this analysis should take place prior to starting to write the protocol and agreed to by the team.

see 2
Study Types and
Study Design

- Nevertheless, the risk-benefit ratio has to be monitored carefully throughout the clinical trial (if possible, by a pharmacovigilance expert); if the ratio turns negative, you have to consider the consequences for the trial continuation.

see 19
Pharmacovigilance

- There has to be a conclusive regulatory consideration from the health authorities regarding the risk-benefit ratio. Only after a positive decision, the investigational IMP can be launched and made available to the pharmaceutical market.

The scientific quality and validity of a clinical trial is primarily determined by the study design. The design must be planned very carefully, because it is difficult to correct inconsistencies afterward. The academic details of planning is not the only determinant of quality – the financial, organizational, logistical and personnel elements of the clinical trial must also be considered in advance by the sponsor-investigator. Early and painstaking considerations in the study design can also prevent influences (so-called bias) from distorting the results of the pre-planned statistical test procedures.

Regulatory Reference

!   ICH GCP Guideline, sections 4.2.1 and 2, 4.7
!   EU Directive 2001/20/EC, Art. 2 a, b, c

Responsibilities

Study Types

In principle, two categories of studies exist: the science differentiates between studies of primary and secondary data. This book does not deepen the topic of secondary data studies, because the research with secondary data only looks at studies that have been completed. The research with primary data means the initiation of a trial with recording of primary data. There are also other differences:

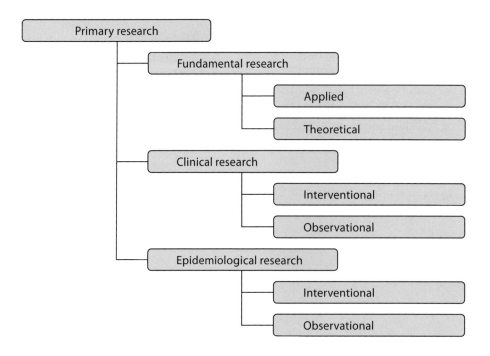

The investigator-initiated trial is a clinical trial involving human subjects; it is always a part of interventional clinical research.

Study Population

To make the right conclusions with regards to the general population using statistical test procedures, the sponsor-investigator has to recruit a representative study population. The principle behind this is that the initial starting position or baseline for the clinical trial is, in essence, the definition of the target group for treatment.

Study Design

The primary aim of a study design is an outcome with a high explanatory power. The gold standard of clinical research is the randomized controlled trial or RCT.

The first step is the **randomization** of the treatment groups, because the experimental units are never identical. By using a random mechanism, the subjects are allocated to the treatment groups. The known and unknown influencing factors on the study results will be equally distributed between study and control group. This method avoids possible bias.

The study is considered controlled when the results of the study population (the active study drug/investigational intervention or verum group) are compared with the results of the non-interventional or control interventional (e.g. placebo, which is considered the most effective measurement) group.

Consider, for example, the so-called crossover design. In this design, the study population and the control group will switch treatments in the middle of the study. This implies that all the participants of the study will get the control intervention and the investigational intervention over two defined periods.

It is advisable to 'blind' (also called 'masking') the study. This type of design means the participants do not know if they are part of the intervention or control group. The influence of expectations and individual behaviour is considered to be minimized in a blinded/masked study.

- **Single-blind:** the participants do not know if they are a part of the intervention or control group.
- **Double-blind:** the participants and the medical staff do not know the allocation.
- **Triple-blind:** neither the participants nor the medical staff, even those that make the statistical evaluation, do not know who is in the intervention or control group.

see 24
Multicentre Trials

To avoid other influences (e.g. environment) the study can be designed as a **multicentre trial**.

Steps for a Good Study Design

The starting point of any clinical trial always should be to pose the question or hypothesis that will be answered by the research. The sponsor-investigator must be clear about the subjects and aims of the project. Given this background, the sponsor-investigator must describe the following points accurately in the **clinical trial protocol**:

see 4
Study Protocol

- Specification of the primary endpoints and, if applicable, of the secondary endpoints that will be measured during the trial
- Description of the type/design of the study, using a schematic representation of trial design, procedures and stages

- Description of the measurements to minimize bias/distortions, including *randomization* and *blinding*
- Description of the trial treatments, the dosage, and dosage regimen of the IMP. This also includes a description of the dosage form, packaging, and labelling of the IMP
- The expected duration of subject participation, and a description of the sequence and duration of all trial periods, including follow-up, if applicable
- Description of the 'stopping rules' or discontinuation criteria for individual subjects, parts of trial and entire trial
- Accountability procedures for the IMP, including the placebo(s) and the comparative product, if applicable
- Maintenance of trial treatment randomization codes and procedures for breaking codes
- The identification of any data to be recorded directly on the Case Report Forms (CRFs) (i.e. when no prior written or electronic record of data exists) and to be considered as source data

Advice – Hints and Tips

A schematic overview, e.g. in form of a chart or table of the study design, is highly desirable because it is not only the sponsor-investigator who works with this information. The medical staff, the responsible authorities and the ethic committee(s) must be able to understand and follow the considerations of the sponsor-investigator's plan.

In the framework of the design and development of masked studies (especially the double-blind), it is necessary to make a randomization plan. This plan is typically made by the biometricians and is the 'top secret' of the trial.

In emergency cases, it may be necessary that the sponsor-investigator must decode the randomization and unblind or unmask the trial.

Regulatory Reference

! ICH GCP Guideline, sections 4.7, 4.11
! EU Directive 2001/20/EC, Art. 16
! ICH Detailed guidance on the collection, verification and presentation of adverse reaction reports arising from clinical trials on medicinal products for human use
! ICH Guideline for clinical safety data management: definitions and standard expedited reporting

During Study

Responsibilities

Breaking the Blind

If complications or serious adverse events (SAEs) occur, the sponsor-investigator must report them immediately to the health authorities and also to the Ethics Committee, if they are unexpected (suspected unexpected serious adverse reaction or SUSAR). A SUSAR must be reported if the complication/SAE is not mentioned in the study protocol as a known side effect or a known event that could occur.

To report a SUSAR, the sponsor-investigator must know the allocation of the treatment group and the all details of the patient. However, in a double-blind trial, not even the sponsor-investigator would know this information because the randomization codes are made by the biometricians. In this case, the sponsor-investigator is allowed and required to break the blind.

Emergency Envelopes

In masked trials, for every participant there exists a sealed 'emergency envelope'. If the sponsor-investigator can no longer ensure the patient's safety without knowing to which treatment group the patient belongs, he must decide whether to open the envelope.

On the envelope is the subject number of the study patient. After opening, the sponsor-investigator learns the allocation of the patient to the treatment group and is only then able to identify any possible correlations to the substances (verum, placebo, comparator, etc.) and the SAE.

After opening the envelopes the sponsor-investigator must document the incident with:
- Name and date
- Kind of emergency

Required Changes in Study Design

If it is necessary to make amendments to the study design, the sponsor- investigator must contact the Ethics Committee.

Advice – Hints and Tips

The sponsor-investigator must be aware of the consequences when unblinding the study. An unnecessary unblinding could affect the objectivity of the trial. It is justified only to unblind or unmask the treatment allocation when a patient experiences a SUSAR or is in any kind of medical emergency. The sponsor-investigator must further ensure that only authorized people know the data of the participant.

In the chapter 'Pharmacovigilance', SUSAR handling is described in detail.

see 19
Pharmacovigilance

Investigational medicinal products (IMPs) are pharmaceutical forms that are tested in a clinical trial for human use. These pharmaceutical forms include pharmaceuticals licensed or not licensed, which are applied to another (currently not licensed) indication or administration form, as well as placebos.

The sponsor-investigator has to ensure that the study site and the participant(s) are provided with enough IMPs. It is very important that the IMPs' manufacturing and handling conform to the local laws.

Regulatory Reference

! EU Guidelines to Good Manufacturing Practice (GMP) Annex 13 Investigational Medicinal Products
! EU Directive 2001/20/EC, Art. 2, Art. 13, Art. 14, Art. 15

Responsibilities

Obtaining IMPs

After the study design and the corresponding IMPs are specified, how the IMPs are obtained has to be ascertained:

- Who delivers the IMP?
- What is the delivery status?
- What specific labelling requirements are defined/required?
- Is a manufacturer allowance needed?

Obtaining from a Manufacturer

If the IMPs were obtained from the original manufacturer, the following items have to be obtained and/or written down in detail:

- Relinquishing the IMP dossier
- Labelling
- Expiration date
- Amount
- Delivery conditions

Obtaining from a Pharmacy

If the IMPs were obtained from a pharmacy, the following aspects have to be written down in detail:

- Amount
- Availability
- Requirement to label
- Pharmacy fee (if any)

Labelling of IMPs

The labelling has to protect the participant, secure the traceability and identification and prevent the invalid usage of the pharmaceutical.

The following items have to be written on the label:

- Name, address and telephone number of the contact person
- Representative or code number to identify the substance
- Route of administration, dosage form, dosage units and, in the case of open trials, the name and the strength of the pharmaceutical
- Study number to identify the study, the sponsor-investigator and the study site
- Participant number
- Application advice
- Hint: use 'Only for Use in Clinical Trial' or similar wording
- Storage conditions
- Expiration date in format mm/yy
- If the IMP is used at the participant's home: 'Store away from children'

Under certain circumstances, items may be placed on a patient card.

Investigational Medicinal Product Dossier

The IMP dossier (IMPD, usually provided by the manufacturing company) contains all the relevant information or a reference to documents, which describe the detailed instructions regarding manufacturing, packaging, shipping and quality control. It must include:

(a) Documents about quality and manufacturing
(b) Import license
(c) Documents about the pharmacological and toxicological tests
(d) Manufacturer allowance
(e) Scheduled labelling
(f) Summarized risk-benefit analyses
(g) Documents of results about clinical trials implemented so far

see 1
Risk-Benefit Analysis

Advice – Hints and Tips

Use symbols and graphics for clarification, as well as other standard warning notices and extra declarations. If the points *(b)*, *(f)* and *(g)* from the IMPD are already provided in the IB, the sponsor-investigator can make a reference to the relevant sections there. Pay attention to the latest version of the IMPD appropriate to the development of the product.

During the clinical trial, the sponsor-investigator has the responsibility for the maintenance of the IMPs. These responsibilities include the reordering and checking of the IMPs to ensure a smooth execution until the end of the study. Additionally, the sponsor-investigator is required to document drug accountability.

Regulatory Reference

! EU Guidelines to GMP Annex 13 Investigational Medicinal Products
! EU Directive 2001/20/EC, Art. 2, Art. 13, Art. 14, Art. 15

Responsibilities

Recalls/Reclamations

Reclamations about the IMPs' quality have to be documented and should be sent to the pharmaceutical manufacturer.

In the case of recalls, it is necessary to coordinate between the sponsor-investigator and the manufacturer. The sponsor-investigator and monitor must be clear about their duties.

Drug Accountability

Drug accountability is the documentation of the:

- Received IMPs, including expiration date and lot number
- Administered amount of the IMP per participant
- Lost amount of the IMP per participant (if any)

Dispensing and redemption of the IMPs is documented in the Drug Accountability Log. It should include the following:

- Name of the sponsor-investigator
- Protocol number and title
- Name of the pharmaceutical
- Date
- Amount
- Manufacturer
- Dose, form and strength of the pharmaceutical
- Lot number
- Study site number
- Signature of the employee responsible for the action

Advice – Hints and Tips

The return or disposal of unused pharmaceuticals is an important responsibility, which must be documented carefully. If the IMP is only to be used by the participant, it is important to educate him/her about the appropriate dosage amount as requested by the study protocol.

In the case of ambulant therapies, it is crucial to document patient compliance.

Forms and Templates

◑ Drug Accountability Log

After terminating or completing a clinical trial, there are several options to document the use of all IMPs. The sponsor-investigator has the responsibility for how to handle cases of destruction, returning the IMP or other possibilities. Furthermore, it has to be ensured that the completion of the drug accountability log is conducted accurately.

Regulatory Reference

! EU Guidelines to GMP Annex 13 Investigational Medicinal Products
! EU Directive 2001/20/EC, Art. 2, Art. 13, Art. 14, Art. 15

Responsibilities

Destruction
The sponsor-investigator is responsible for the IMP – in particular, for the destruction of unused pharmaceuticals.

The delivery use and destruction of IMPs must be written down in detail. The balance has to be made up for every audit period. All IMPs must be accounted.

The destruction of the IMPs has to be proved with a dated and signed document. Furthermore, it must contain:

- Lot-number
- Participant-number
- Destroyed amount or complying traceability

Drug Accountability
The monitor's task at the end of the study is to compare the trial notes to the Drug Accountability Log. If it is necessary, the destruction or redemption of the IMPs has to be initiated by the monitor.

see 23
Monitoring

After Study

Returning

The returning of IMPs must be in compliance with procedures, which were agreed to beforehand. Returned pharmaceuticals should be discernible as such and stored separately.

Advice – Hints and Tips

To destroy IMPs, a written approval of the sponsor-investigator is required. Their destruction has to be traceable, such that all actions have to be written down, signed by authorized study staff and dated.

Forms and Templates

↻ Drug Destruction Log

Before Initiation

The study protocol is the basis of a clinical trial. The protocol addresses the quality, the ethical feasibility and the objectivity regarding the efficacy of the IMP.

The responsible authorities can only give approval when the operations and methodology are described exactly. For the clinical trial protocol, this means the intentions must be consistent, methodologically sound and every step repeatable for another research team.

Regulatory Reference

! ICH GCP Guideline, Chapter 6
! Declaration of Helsinki, B. 13, B. 14
! EU Directive 2001/20/EC, Art. 2 h, Art. 6.3 c, Art. 10 a, Art. 11 c

Responsibilities

Formal Requirements of the Study Protocol

The development of the protocol can be cumbersome; the sponsor-investigator must rely on his/her team, for instance, to collect all the important information (e.g. the required sample size from the statistician or essential laboratory data from the biochemist).

The authorities provide the sections and organization of the protocol. The main sections are:

1. General information
2. Background information
3. Trial objectives and purpose
4. Trial design
5. Selection and withdrawal of subjects
6. Treatment of subjects
7. Assessment of efficacy
8. Assessment of safety
9. Statistics
10. Direct access to source data/ documents
11. Quality control and quality assurance
12. Ethics
13. Data handling and record keeping
14. Financing and insurance
15. Publication policy
16. Supplements

see 1
Risk-Benefit Analysis

see 2
Study Types and Study Design

see 10
Informed Consent

see 22
Quality

see 17
Data Management

see 12
Insurance

Keeping with the protocol outline development and its required structure is not easy. In this chapter's section 'Forms and Templates', the sponsor-investigator can use the template of a protocol outline for additional guidance.

Responsible Authorities

After writing the study protocol, the sponsor-investigator must send the completed document to the Ethics Committee(s) and health authorities to receive the approval for the study initiation.

Advice – Hints and Tips

The sponsor-investigator should not assume changes in the study protocol could be made a priori. Each change must be handled with care and, possibly, the amended protocol may need to be approved again.

Clinical trials often have tight time schedules. Bearing this in mind, every change in the study protocol needs adequate time to be implemented, time which could be better spent in getting the protocol right **before** submission.

Forms and Templates

 Protocol Template
(http://www.nia.nih.gov/NR/rdonlyres/57864169-734F-4B05-9DC0-A7B2E38C5A55/0/
ProtocolTemplate_11_12_2007_Final.doc; accessed January 19, 2011)

After getting the approval of the Ethics Committee(s) and the health authorities, the sponsor-investigator must maintain the study protocol regarding its timeliness. Accordingly, the regulatory references allow changes only under well-defined conditions. The amendments of the trial protocol can be classified as either a change in **substantial** or **nonsubstantial** documents. Special forms are required for **urgent** (and substantial) amendments.

Regulatory Reference

! ICH GCP Guideline, Chapter 6
! EU Directive 2001/20/EC, Art. 10
! EU Detailed guidance for the request for authorisation of a clinical trial on a medicinal product for human use to the competent authorities, notification of substantial amendments and declaration of the end of the trial

Responsibilities

Labelling the Amendment
The initial approval of the Ethics Committee and the health authorities is based upon the information contained in the clinical trial application, but does not include any later changes which may have been made. In case of any amendments, they must be attached to the latest version of the protocol. All amendment forms must be signed by the sponsor-investigator. All modifications to the protocol shall be added as an amendment and must be labelled with the date, initials of the authorized person and the signature in the original document.

Procedure for Notification

Substantial amendments must be reported to the competent health authorities and Ethics Committee(s) to obtain approval, or more often, an agreement of the changes.

see 13
Health Authority Approval

For the 'Notification of a Substantial Amendment Form', a template is available in the chapter 'Health Authority Approvals'. A covering letter with a description of the modification and the relevant information related to the original application with a signature of the sponsor-investigator should be added to the notification form. An overview of the impact on the risk-benefit-analysis must also be included.

In contrast, *non-substantial amendments* do not require notification but must be recorded with the date of the change.

Advice – Hints and Tips

- The Ethics Committee gives an ethical opinion on the amendment within (not more than) **35 days** from the date of receiving the correct notice of amendment.
- Where a negative opinion is given, the sponsor-investigator may submit a modified amendment. The Ethics Committee will give an opinion on the modified amendment within **14 days** after receipt.

Forms and Templates

◑ Protocol Amendment Covering Letter
◑ Protocol Amendment Template

The study protocol and amendments, if any, also represent the basis of the Final Study Report at the end of the trial. The main topics of both documents are generally identical; this usually makes the necessary detailed and explanatory writing more comfortable for the sponsor-investigator.

see 26
Final Study Report and Publication

Regulatory Reference

! ICH GCP Guideline, Chapter 6.16
! ICH GCP Guideline E3: Note for Guidance on Structure and Content of Clinical Study Reports

After Study

Responsibilities

Study Completion

Within a year after the completion of the clinical aspects of a study, a summary of the study report must be sent to the Ethics Committee and the competent Health Authorities.

Often, the last regular ward round of the last participant (last patient, last visit) determines the completion date of the study, and therefore, of the protocol.

Further Actions

The sponsor-investigator has the responsibility to complete the trial in the manner stated in the study protocol. Responsibilities include the statistical analysis, data management, archiving, etc. as well as taking care of the observation of the study participants after the completion (patient follow-up period).

For more detailed instructions, please review the 'After Study' sections of the following chapters:

- IMPs (in particular, handling and disposal)
- Ethics
- Trial Master File
- Documentation and Data Management (archiving)
- Pharmacovigilance (care of the participants in subsequent study phases)
- Quality (standard operating procedures, etc.)
- Biometry (statistical evaluation)
- Final Study Report

see
After Study sections
3. Investigational Medicinal Products
14. Ethics
15. Trial Master File, Updating and Archiving
16. Documentation
17. Data Management
19. Pharmacovigilance
22. Quality
24. Biometry

Before Initiation

A **Case Report Form (CRF)** is a printed or electronic document that is created and used in clinical trial research to capture standardised clinical data from each patient separately and to transfer it to Data Management.

see 17
Data Management

The structure of the CRF is comparable with a questionnaire that contains all of the protocol-designated information (also including (serious) adverse events) and which is in compliance with regulatory requirements, recorded by the sponsor-investigator on every study visit. In addition, CRFs ensure an accurate documentation as well as high quality of data and are defined as one of the essential documents of the **Trial Master File (TMF)**.

see 15
Trial Master File,
Updating and
Archiving

Regulatory Reference

!   ICH GCP Guideline, Chapters 1.11, 8.2.2, 8.2.7
!   Society for Clinical Data Management: Good Clinical Data Management Practices 2009

Responsibilities

Prior to the development of the final CRF, the following steps should be followed, so that possible inconsistencies and handling errors can be avoided from the outset.

Accuracy of the Study Protocol

First of all, the sponsor-investigator and the persons involved in the draft of the study protocol must confirm its completeness and elaborateness, such that the required content of the finalized protocol can be transferred into CRF sheets.

Frequently, it is recommended to begin with the creation of the CRF at the same time as developing the protocol.

CRF-Structure

The CRF must be in accordance with the protocol and should reflect it precisely, so this document has to consist of particular forms or entry areas to be modified:

- Study Identification
  (Study Number, Logo, Abbreviated Title)
- Patient Identification
  (Number, Site Number)
- Guidance
  (Headline)

        } Header

- Assurance of Informed Consent
- Date of Screening
  (containing inclusion/exclusion criteria)
- Demography and Physical Examination
  (containing age, sex, pregnancy test, etc.)
- Concomitant Diagnosis and Medication
- Patient's Diaries or Quality of Life-Questionnaires
  in the order of their appointments
- Treatment
  (containing efficacy parameters, etc.)
- Changes in Concomitant Diagnosis and Medication
  (during the study)
- Remarks
  (during the process of treatment)
- Premature Termination
  (including given reasons, if appropriate)
- Scheduled Termination
- Pregnancy Surveillance
  (in case of a patient's current pregnancy)
- Adverse Events
- Serious Adverse Events Report
  (do not forget, very important)

Principal part

see 19
Pharmacovigilance

- Version Information
  (version, creation date)

Footer

CRF Design and Extension

The CRF design should be implemented in an attractive, clear and unambiguous form, otherwise, extensions and misinterpretations might cause data faults on the basis of confusion.

It is required that every CRF sheet implies explicit queries, clear instructions, prompts and controlling fields (that allow the efficient and complete coding of data for processing and analysis) in combination with text fields for the sponsor-investigator's entries.

If your CRF is in a paper-based form, optionally every sheet (except pure-tip sheets) should be printed on non-carbon paper (NCR paper) with corresponding page numbers, so that copies of the original sheets can remain in chronological order with the study site and are not lost completely in case of loss or missing CRF sheets.

Advice – Hints and Tips

- Bear in mind the CRF needs to be finalized (with version control and approval from each study site) and be a useable form **before** the sponsor-investigator starts enrolling patients into the clinical trial.
- Ensure that on the CRF, personal data is not identifiable; use screening numbers and randomization numbers (i.e. in a randomized study) instead of real names.
- Remember: do not make use of your printed sample CRF until you have checked the conformity, contents and completeness with the protocol.
- Usually, paper-based CRFs should be stored in an environment with regulated access authority.
- If you want to enter data electronically *(eCRF/Remote Data Capture (RDC))* with the assistance of online data capture software instead of paper CRFs, please validate your electronic system correctly in the presence of an IT specialist; likewise, take universal precautions such as password protection and firewall security.

Forms and Templates

Several freely available examples illustrate how a CRF could be meaningfully designed; the level of detail reflects the protocol and can be clearly followed.

- Adverse Events Form
- Prior and Concomitant Med
- Protocol Deviations Core Form
- Serious Adverse Events Form
- Study Completion
- Visit Checklist
- Inclusion Exclusion Core Form
- Demographics Form
- Medical History
- Medical History Conventional
- Vital Signs
- Physical Exam

(all documents from http://www.nia.nih.gov/ResearchInformation/CTtoolbox/forms.htm #admin; accessed January 19, 2011)

After the CRF is compiled, approved and finalized as the latest version, it can be used to collect clinical data during the course of the clinical trial – commencing with the enrolment of the first patient – according to the protocol and in compliance with regulatory requirements.

Only the sponsor-investigator and authorized staff (authorization should be documented) are allowed to perform written entries into the provided (text) fields on the CRF sheets.

Regulatory Reference

! ICH GCP Guideline, Chapters 2.10, 4.9.1-4.9.3, 6.4.9, 8.3.2, 8.3.14–8.3.15
! Society for Clinical Data Management: Good Clinical Data Management Practices 2009

Responsibilities

Accuracy and Completeness of Medical Documentation

Ensure that all recordings in the CRF or in the required reports (e.g. with the appearance of SAEs) are:

- Devoid of patient name (i.e. anonymous)
- Exact (for accurate reporting, interpretation and verification)
- Current
- Complete
- Consistent
- Legible (also on the NCR paper, if available)
- Written in the same language as the CRF was designed, using a permanent ball-point pen

Either the study nurse or the sponsor-investigator may complete the CRF. CRF completion should be done as soon as possible with regard to the date when data were obtained (i.e. the study subject's visit at the clinic). If the study nurse completes the CRF, this task must have been already properly delegated on the delegation of authority list provided by the sponsor-investigator.

The sponsor-investigator is still responsible for confirming the correctness and completeness of the data in the CRF through her/his signature. This confirmation cannot be delegated.

Even if tests or examinations could not be performed due to a patient's poor compliance, those failed visits have to be registered accurately on the provided sheets and all the appropriate (text) fields should be crossed out, so that it is absolutely impossible to add any entries later.

Corrections and Changes

The sponsor-investigator should take care if any corrections, additions or changes to the CRF must be done in accordance with ICH GCP.

- Changes to the CRF: any changes made to the initial entry must be traceable and properly dated and initialled. A justification may be included whenever it is appropriate: it is not always required.
- Corrections may not cover the original entry (please cross out each wrong listing with a straight line and correct it, as previously mentioned).

see 23
Monitoring

Delivery of CRFs to Monitoring

Within the scope of long ongoing clinical trials in particular, it is recommended to transfer individual sheets or whole recorded CRFs at defined intervals to Monitoring to prevent the loss of CRF data; likewise, this ensures a prompt and continuous data capture by Data Management.

Advice – Hints and Tips

- Ensure that all authorized staff receives instructions about the correct entry and handling of CRFs to prevent loss or inaccurate documentation.
- Bear in mind that superficial or inaccurate completion of the CRF ultimately leads to data faults, which are time-consuming to be corrected afterward.
- Make sure that all essential signatures (also needed in case of changes or corrections) required in the CRF exist and are given by authorized staff.
- Data reported on the CRF that are derived from the protocol and source documents should also be consistent with those documents (any changes to the protocol also have to be reflected in the CRF and vice versa).
- Serious Adverse Events Reports (with the study's EudraCT number) must be completed explicitly and reported immediately to the relevant pharmaceutical company (i.e. study IMP manufacturer).

see 8
EudraCT

see 19
Pharmacovigilance

After Study

Finally, when the study ends or is terminated, all the clinical information on each patient required by the protocol should be reported accurately on the CRFs without any exceptions.

Regulatory Reference

- ! ICH GCP Guideline, Chapters 5.18.4, 8.2–8.3
- ! Society for Clinical Data Management: Good Clinical Data Management Practices 2009

Responsibilities

Transferring of Remaining CRF Sheets
The sponsor-investigator must ensure that after completion of the clinical trial, all outstanding CRFs are transferred to Monitoring.

Correcting of Non-Conforming CRF Entries
The sponsor-investigator has to be informed by Monitoring about any illegible, omitted, incorrect (e.g. protocol deviation) or inconsistent CRF entries, likewise, in the context of *query management*.

see 23
Monitoring

see 17
Data Management

Those corrections must be made by the sponsor-investigator or by an authorized staff member directly on the CRF (and NCR paper), including all corrections, deletions and additions, which have to be:

- dated
- explained (if not self-evident)
- signed

by the responsible corrector and endorsed by the sponsor-investigator.

Destruction of Unused CRFs

With the decision of the sponsor-investigator, unused CRFs should be destroyed.

Archiving of CRFs

CRFs and all appropriate forms should remain at the study site to be archived for a definite period.

see 15
Trial Master File,
Updating and
Archiving

Advice – Hints and Tips

- Make sure that no CRFs/individual CRF sheets are withheld from Monitoring.
- Bear in mind that the often used adhesive post-it® notes are not conforming to ICH GCP.
- Ensure that all corrections and changes made on the CRFs are dated and signed (using a ball-point pen) by an authorized corrector, and endorsed by the sponsor-investigator.
- Ensure that all CRFs remain at your study site and are properly archived according to ICH GCP.

6 Financing

The sponsor-investigator should take heed of these two expressions: 'no cash, no bash' and 'time is money'.

A clinical trial provokes huge costs. If the sponsor or sponsor-investigator does not have enough money for the study, he/she cannot pay for all the required materials, facilities, IMPs, and other study expenses.

In the worst case, the study will not be compliant to the Study Protocol and has to be interrupted or cancelled.

Regulatory Reference

! ICH GCP Guideline, Chapters 5.9, 6.14 and 8.2.4

Responsibilities

There are no specific policies regarding study costs and finances. However, it is highly recommended that special care be taken to ensure there is a signed contract between the sponsor-investigator and the investor(s) about the funding situation as needed. A finance plan must be created and presented in the study protocol.

Advice – Hints and Tips

Before the trial starts, ensure that there are enough financial resources to run the study to its completion, including publication.

All expenses should be calculated with a reasonable tolerance. Bear in mind that a lack of liquidation might have undesirable consequences and impact the study conduct.

Due to the nature of investigative clinical trials, it is strongly recommended to set aside reserves for unforeseeable events and issues to complete the study. Try to estimate all the expenses that can originate during the study; look for budget references in other similar studies in relation to the expenses to get a keen sense of estimating your own study costs and to create your own finance and investment plan.

Many institutions, people, and companies stand to benefit if your study is successful, thus, most investors will be cooperative. In general, a clinical study requires financing for:

- Facilities
- Technical requirements
- Medical products/medical devices
- Personnel
- Patients
- Contracts and approvals
- Insurances
- Documentation and administration
- Unscheduled delays and activities

Possible investors include the pharmaceutical company of your IMP. Quite often, the pharmaceutical company will provide the IMP(s) to you for free. Try to get subsidies from your government or other research institutions or societies.

You may transfer financial tasks to third parties if you do not feel comfortable to manage the financial details of the trial. However, bear in mind the more you outsource, the more you transfer your sponsor-responsibilities to other parties.

Operational Instructions

- The sponsor-investigator should create a detailed finance and investment plan (with the support of the investor, if available).
- The investor and the sponsor-investigator should sign a contract that is based on the finance and investment plan above.
- All financing-related documents should be placed in the Trial Master File (TMF).

During Study

It is often the case that some procedures or objectives related to the clinical trial change during the study. As a consequence, the costs can increase immediately.

What should the sponsor-investigator do if some costs in the finance structure and plan are significantly shifted?

Regulatory Reference

! ICH GCP Guideline, Chapters 5.9, 6.14 and 8.2.4

Responsibilities

Financial liquidation has to be backed by the sponsor-investigator. For this reason, there are no regulatory policies. It is clear that the study cannot be finished if there are not enough resources.

Advice – Hints and Tips

Financial plans should consider any kind of changes during the study. The financial plan and any revisions to it should be checked carefully before changes are implemented. The financial plan should be kept up-to-date at all times by the sponsor-investigator in order to 'hold the purse strings' and to manage the budget. In case of financial issues, try to find new/further financial sources as soon as possible. Try to overcome such challenges or unforeseeable huge costs by renegotiating with your investor.

Retain the receipts for all expenses made in the study. It makes sense to compare your estimated costs with your effective costs. This will be a good indicator whether you need to save on non-essential expenses or you have residual money.

If a patient is harmed, the insurance company of your study may also provide financial compensation.

see 12
Insurance

Operational Instructions

You should:
- Create a consolidated financial statement to show all the costs originated during the clinical trial (periodically, if possible)
- Put all additional financial documents, receipts or cost-related material in the TMF
- Make receipts for all disbursements, obtain signatures for the receipt of disbursements from the beneficiary, and get receipts for all expenses

To conduct a clinical trial, the sponsor-investigator and the study nurse must follow certain rules and the trial site must meet specifications, in accordance with GCP Guidelines.

The qualifications of the sponsor-investigator are as important as those of the trial site. The qualifications and the professionalism of the doctors and the non-medical staff involved are also relevant.

Regulatory Reference

! ICH GCP Guideline, Chapters 4 .1, 4.2, 5.6, 5.7
! EU Directive 2001/20/EC, Art. 3.3

Responsibilities

To take part in a clinical trial, certain regulations are mandatory for the sponsor-investigator(s), the study nurse, and the trial site. Furthermore, all study staff must act in accordance to the GCP guidelines.

Sponsor-Investigator(s)

The sponsor-investigator must submit to the Ethics Committee his/her current curriculum vitae dated and signed, including name, office address, professional experience, other qualifications, completed studies, as well as education, training and qualifications, which are required by law.

see 14
Ethics

This verification of qualifications is important because the sponsor-investigator is responsible for the entire clinical trial and all clinical trial-related medical decisions.

see 4
Study Protocol

The sponsor-investigator must thoroughly know the exact protocol to implement the trial and must also understand the use of the product. The sponsor-investigator usually must provide proof of 2 years' experience with clinical trials and GCP.

Another duty of the sponsor-investigator is to inform the trial subject about the study and to notify the family physician about the trial, if the subject so desires.

Study Nurse

The study nurse acts as an assistant to the sponsor-investigator. He/she must submit a topical CV, showing function and qualifications, including training and clinical trial experience.

Similar to the sponsor-investigator, he/she is obliged to act in accordance with the protocol and GCP.

The study nurse must be provided with accurate and detailed information about the trial (e.g. in dealing with SAEs, SUSARs and the obligation to notify the authorities).

The sponsor-investigator must explain and discuss any additional duties with the study nurse.

Study Site

To implement a trial successfully, the study site should also be chosen for optimal qualifications, such as supportive technical equipment, adequate facility for storage of the investigational product, suitable rooms and availability of appropriate equipment.

Additional key factors are the availability, experience and qualifications of emergency care staff, and/or the distance to another hospital with emergency care facilities.

The number of trial participants should not exceed the capacity of the study site.

Advice – Hints and Tips

- If you do not have GCP training yet, bear in mind that there are online systems available for distance learning.
- Use the 'Delegation of Authority' Form; it will help you with the delegation of the tasks.
- At all times, it is important to be knowledgeable about your proposed study, particularly with regard to the:
  - Study protocol
  - SAEs
  - SUSARs
  - Storage of investigational product and other documents

Forms and Templates

◑ Curriculum Vitae / Qualification
◑ Delegation of Authority

In general, an investigator is the person who is responsible for the conduct of the clinical trial at a trial site. He/she is also the responsible leader, if a trial is conducted by a team of individuals at the study site.

In an investigator-initiated trial, it is the sponsor-investigator who takes the ultimate responsibility for the trial. Consequently, he/she is responsible for a continual risk/benefit assessment and, furthermore, is the one who is able to stop or interrupt the trial if he/she cannot longer take the responsibility for continuation due to e.g. safety reasons.

Regulatory Reference

! ICH GCP Guideline, Chapter 4.3

During Study

Responsibilities

Sponsor-Investigator

The sponsor-investigator is responsible for a protocol-compliant trial and might decide to terminate or interrupt the trial due to specific reasons such as safety concerns identified during the course of the trial.

The sponsor-investigator is also responsible for the:

see 15
Trial Master File,
Updating and
Archiving

- IMP
- Indication under study
- Study management
- Handling of information/data
- Compliance with the study protocol
- Randomisation method
- Handling of SAEs and SUSARs
- Communication with Ethics Committee(s)
- Medical supply of the subjects

In addition, he/she needs to keep everyone up-to-date and must directly communicate accurate information.

The sponsor-investigator authenticates with a signature that he/she takes note of any new documents; therefore, documents can be inserted in an ongoing process.

Advice – Hints and Tips

If new physicians or assistants join the study team, they must be announced immediately to the Ethics Committee with their CV and other essential details.

see 14
Ethics

Every clinical trial conducted in Europe must be announced to the **European Medicines Agency (EMA)** using the European Union Drug Regulating Authorities Clinical Trials (EudraCT) database system. The EudraCT database comprises all clinical trials conducted in the European Union since 1 May 2004.

The health authorities of the Member States, which grant the approval and the supervision of clinical trials, use this database, created and maintained by the EMA. Another task of the EudraCT is to provide sponsor-investigators with a grasp of the basics of the approval application, the recommended statement from the study site's Ethics Committee, information on the termination of a clinical study, as well as hints to carry out inspections.

The assigned **EudraCT Number** is the central identification for a clinical trial in Europe and is to be stated in all correspondence with authorities and the Ethics Committee.

Regulatory Reference

! Detailed guidance on the collection, verification and presentation of adverse reaction reports arising from clinical trials on medicinal products for human use
! Detailed guidance for the request for authorisation of a clinical trial on a medicinal product for human use to the competent authorities, notification of substantial amendments and declaration of the end of the trial
! Detailed guidance on the application format and documentation to be submitted in an application for an Ethics Committee opinion on the clinical trial on medicinal products for human use
! Detailed guidance on the European clinical trials database (EudraCT database)

Responsibilities

Request for a EudraCT Number
Prior the submission of the clinical trial to the health authority, the sponsor-investigator must visit the website of European Clinical Trials Database to obtain a unique EudraCT Number (please review the Operational Instructions for detailed information).

Labelling
The EudraCT Number is strongly recommended to (in most cases, is required to) be used prominently in the following:

- All covering letter headings as well as other (including electronic) correspondence with the Competent Authority
- All of the documents sent to the Ethics Committee before commencement of a clinical trial
- The actual Clinical Trial Application (required field)
- As one of the required minimum criteria for the initial **expedited reporting** of SUSARs, the specification of the EudraCT number acts as the study protocol number
- The first page of an adverse event report
- On the label of the IMP (required)
- On the study protocol (required)

Advice – Hints and Tips

For specific information, review the up-to-date EudraCT User Manual and the FAQ guide:

- https://eudract.ema.europa.eu/docs/userGuides/EudraCT_Public_User_Manual.pdf (accessed November 2010)
- https://eudract.ema.europa.eu/docs/userGuides/EudraCT_Public_FAQ.pdf (accessed November 2010)

Operational Instructions

The process of obtaining a EudraCT Number includes the following 5 steps:

1. Visit the website of European Clinical Trials Database: https://eudract.emea.europa.eu/

2. Click the following button 'Access to EudraCT Application' on this page.

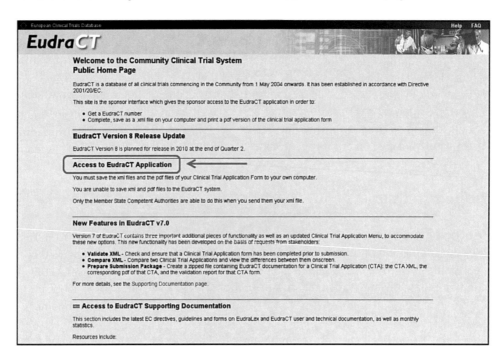

3. Next, a new page, 'Welcome to EudraCT' is shown.

4. Choose 'Step 1' for applying for a security code for a single clinical trial, which is **valid only for 24 hours**.

Next, you have to specify your *name* and *e-mail address*.

EudraCT Number Step 1

The first stage in the process is to obtain an authenticated security code. This security code will be sent to the e-mail address specified by you, the requestor, on the form, and is needed in order to complete the EudraCT Number request. The security code is valid for one EudraCT Number only and expires after 24 hours.

(**Apply for Security Code**)

5. 'Step 2' in the process stands for the application of a EudraCT Number that will be sent to the given e-mail address and **will never expire** once it is issued.

On receipt of the security code, the following information is necessary for the preservation of the EudraCT Number:

- Name of the organisation of the applicant
- Address of the organisation of the applicant
- Name of the sponsor-investigator
- E-mail address of the sponsor-investigator for the dispatch of the EudraCT Number

EudraCT Number Step 2

This is the main EudraCT Number request that allows the requestor to obtain a EudraCT Number that will provide the unique reference for the Clinical Trial. The EudraCT number will be sent to the e-mail address specified by you, the requestor, on the form.

(**Apply for EudraCT Number**)

European Clinical Trials Database (Public Site)　　　help　　faq　　contact

EudraCT
Version 7.0.3

Get EudraCT Number

All fields marked with '*' must be completed in all requests.

If you are requesting the EudraCT number as an individual, then you may leave the 'Requestor's organisation name' empty. In this case the system will copy your 'Requestor's name' into the 'Requestor's organisation name' box. You must include your contact details in the 'Requestor's organisation town/city' and 'Requestor's organisation country' boxes.

When you have completed the form, use the 'Get EudraCT Number' button and an e-mail with a EudraCT Number will be sent to the e-mail address entered. If you want to cancel this application for a EudraCT number, use the 'Cancel' button which will take you back .

Requestor's organisation name:

Requestor's organisation town/city(*):

Requestor's organisation country(*):

Sponsor's protocol code number(*):

Requestor name(*):

E-mail to which the EudraCT number will be sent(*):

Enter the security code sent earlier(*):

Is it anticipated that this EudraCT Number will be used for a Clinical Trial contained in a Paediatric Investigation Plan (PIP)? (*)　　○ Yes ○ No

Is it anticipated that this EudraCT Number will be used for a Clinical Trial conducted in a third country (outside of the EU/EEA)? (*)　　○ Yes ○ No

Please select the Member States where it is anticipated that the trial will be run:

AUSTRIA: ☐	BELGIUM: ☐	BULGARIA: ☐
CYPRUS: ☐	CZECH REPUBLIC: ☐	DENMARK: ☐
ESTONIA: ☐	FINLAND: ☐	FRANCE: ☐
GERMANY: ☐	GREECE: ☐	HUNGARY: ☐
ICELAND: ☐	IRELAND: ☐	ITALY: ☐
LATVIA: ☐	LIECHTENSTEIN: ☐	LITHUANIA: ☐
LUXEMBOURG: ☐	MALTA: ☐	NETHERLANDS: ☐
NORWAY: ☐	POLAND: ☐	PORTUGAL: ☐
ROMANIA: ☐	SLOVAKIA: ☐	SLOVENIA: ☐
SPAIN: ☐	SWEDEN: ☐	UNITED KINGDOM: ☐

Get EudraCT Number　　Cancel

Important: The completed Clinical Trial Application Form must be stored before and during the study treatment process. It is recommended to store the XML file on an external medium for long-term storage (e.g. CD-ROM).

Optional:
6. After receiving the number, it is possible to look up the details of the Clinical Trial Application Form.

Create New Clinical Trial Application
Once you have the EudraCT Number and wish to enter Clinical Trial Application details please use this link.

(Click here to create a new Clinical Trial Application)　←

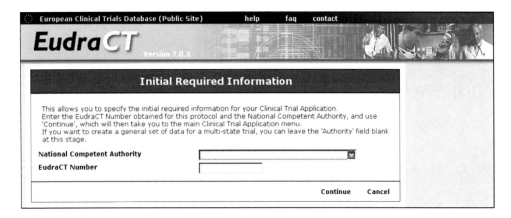

Finally, the Clinical Trial Application Form should be stored in XML- and PDF-format on a CD-ROM and must be submitted to the Competent Authorities.

Please note: In the version 7 of EudraCT shown, you must save the XML files and the PDF files of your Clinical Trial Application Form to your own computer. You are unable to save XML and PDF files to the EudraCT system. Only the Member States' Competent Authorities are able to do this when you send them your XML file.

Before Initiation

This chapter describes the handling of contracts specifically for investigator-initiated clinical studies.

Regulatory Reference

! ICH GCP Guideline, 1.17, 4.1–4.6, 5.1.2, 5.1.4, 5.9

Responsibilities

The sponsor-investigator has to ensure that the contract between him and the relevant company, e.g. the Contract Research Organisation (CRO) or the pharmaceutical company, contains the following items, as far as appropriate, for the relevant type of contract.

- Sponsor's name and address
- CRO's name and address (if applicable)
- Protocol title and number
- Indemnification language
- Confidentiality agreement (if not in a separate document)
- Estimated start and finish dates of the trial
- Estimated number of subjects expected to enrol from the study site (can also specify for each study site in a multicentre trial)
- Budget information and payment schedule, including terms for delays and termination of the study
- The definition of a 'completed' subject (i.e. fully-paid)
- Description of the reimbursement policies and process for study subjects who experience an adverse event (AE) or who are injured while participating in the study
- A list of the responsibilities assigned to the study site
- A statement of whose Standard Operating Procedures (SOPs) will be followed (i.e. from the sponsor, the CRO, or the study site)
- Publication rights
- Data ownership rights

In addition, the **Research Director** and the **Legal Department** should review the integrity of the abovementioned aspects.

Advice – Hints and Tips

Please note that all agreements have to be approved by the Legal Department, a representative of the company and by you.

If the company is preparing the agreement, two originals will be prepared and sent to you for signature. A copy will be retained in the interim; this copy will be discarded when the signed original is returned. You have to sign both originals, keep one of them, and return the other to the company.

Any contractual agreement must be in place before any subjects are enrolled in the study.

Forms and Templates

The scheme listed below shows the characteristic parts of a model agreement with the pharmaceutical company supplying the study's investigational (new) drug or IMP.

Purpose and Objective of Agreement

At first, your role is defined, e.g. as sponsor-investigator to conduct a research project involving the pharmaceutical company's compound drug(s). This role is designated in accordance with the terms defined in the protocol of the study and the specific ICH GCP definitions.

The study will be performed under the supervision and responsibility of you, the sponsor-investigator.

Protocol

The study is carried out exactly in accordance with the terms of the corresponding protocol. In case the manufacturer only provides the IMP, the company may wish to review the protocol prior to its implementation. Any amendments or modifications must be in writing and agreed upon by both parties (as appropriate).

see 4
Study Protocol

Investigator's Brochure (IB)

You must be familiar with this document before the study commences. The pharmaceutical company should answer any product-related questions that may emerge from the study site(s).

see 11
Investigator's Brochure/Summary of Product Characteristics

Sponsor-Investigator's Obligations

You should carry out the study in accordance with any and all applicable rules and regulations (such as the Declaration of Helsinki and the Good Practices ICH GCP, Good Laboratory Practice [GLP] and/or GMP) as well as in strict observance of the study protocol. Furthermore, another obligation is to agree to submit drafts of all ***substantial amendments*** (e.g. substantial protocol amendments) to the health authorities and to the Ethics Committee in a timely manner.

see 17
Data Management

see 21
Source Data Verification

Other tasks include being in charge of implementing the study and being responsible for any study-related activities such as monitoring, data management (e.g. data entry, validation), auditing, intermediary and/or final data analysis, and preparation of the final study report and the final publication.

see 23
Monitoring

see 26
Final Study Report and Publication

Confidentiality

Prior to or during the course of the study, the company may provide you with confidential information, including but not limited to the IB. The information may not be disclosed to anyone else without prior approval of the company in writing.

An additional task might be to take any reasonable steps so that your collaborators will be under the same confidential obligation.

Ethics Committee Approval

Written approval for the protocol and all amendment(s) – similar to the content of the patient information form – must be obtained by you from a properly constituted Ethics Committee (e.g. at the study site), according to the local law prior to the commencement of the study.

see 14
Ethics

Clinical Trial Application

A clinical trial application (CTA) in accordance to local regulations must be submitted to the national health authority by the sponsor-investigator. You are responsible for ensuring that all requirements are met in accordance to local regulations for clinical trials.

Adverse Events

It is possible that you have to provide a copy of any correspondence regarding safety information (including SAE submissions) between you and the competent health authorities to the *pharmaceutical company's drug safety department*. Furthermore, it is not unusual that there exists a specific time period for reporting and for creating *periodic information reports*.

see 19
Pharmacovigilance

Early Termination

You must be aware, that for some reasons, the study may be stopped prior to its conclusion. The pharmaceutical company could reserve the right to terminate the agreement (e.g. in the event of irregularities in the method by which the study is carried out, or, if necessary, in the interests of the health of the trial subjects).

Moreover, a further clause should imply that the company compensates you pro-rata if the study is unilaterally terminated earlier than this agreement, or if you are unable to complete the study for reasons beyond your control.

Drug Usage

The pharmaceutical company must agree to provide the sponsor-investigator with the required units of drug, with the corresponding dosage for the number of clinical subjects.

Publication of Data

In this part, you may have the requirement that it is not allowed to publish or disclose information concerning the trial to any third party without the express written permission of the drug company.

Exclusion of Liability

The pharmaceutical company is not liable for a misapplication of the drug by the study participants. *However, the liability for the quality, any defect in the manufacture, or the failure of the drug to meet product specifications will remain with the company.*

Indemnity

You may use the following text directly in your contract:

In consideration of the sponsor-investigator entering into the agreement, the pharmaceutical company undertakes to indemnify and keep indemnified, the sponsor-investigator ('the one whose indemnified') from and against any loss, damage, reasonable expense (including reasonable legal costs and expenses) or legal liability ('loss') suffered or incurred by the one whose indemnified, arising from any claims or proceedings made or brought against the one whose indemnified and directly caused by an unlawful, wrongful, fraudulent or negligent act or omission of the pharmaceutical company, or any company personnel in connection with the study.

Insurance

You have to ensure that all necessary insurance required in order to perform the study are in existence and valid. Furthermore, you have to provide the company with a copy of the relevant insurance policy and to communicate any changes of the relevant insurance coverage with the company.

see 12
Insurance

Finance

For the conduct of the clinical trial, the pharmaceutical company may provide financial support for the total or for a specific amount. Also, an agreed schedule for the payment with the payee and address with a time frame for the payment should be listed in the Study Protocol.

see 6
Financing

Execution

Optionally, the contract can include an 'entire agreement' statement, such as the following:

This agreement constitutes the entire agreement between the parties with respect to this subject matter and supersedes all previous proposals, both oral and written, negotiations, representations, commitments, writings, and all other communications between the parties. This agreement may not be released, discharged or modified except by an instrument signed by the parties.

The informed consent is the most important document for the protection of human subjects in clinical trials. If the patient disagrees with the informed consent, he/she cannot participate in the study. During the trial, it also protects the sponsor-investigator from legal consequences if the patient is harmed. On the other hand, the patient is instructed about all his rights and duties, as well as possible risks and foreseeable adverse events. It can be used as a contract between the sponsor-investigator and the participant. Unlawful offenses against the directives result in a personal liability of the sponsor-investigator.

see 19
Pharmacoviligance

Regulatory Reference

!   ICH GCP Guideline, 4.8
!   EU Directive 2001/20/EC, Art. 2, Art. 3, Art. 4, Art. 5, Art. 6

Responsibilities

Before the study starts, the sponsor-investigator guarantees that a form for the informed consent is created in accordance with all the items mentioned below. This document will only become effective after the patient receives, reads, dates and signs the form. The sponsor-investigator has to sign it after the participant.

Items that must be explained in the Informed Consent Form:

- Explanation that the clinical trial is part of research
- Treatment during the trial
- Probability for randomized allocation to a study group
- Course of events and study design
- Rights and duties of participants
- Experimental aspects of the trial
- Foreseeable risks for participants as well as for embryo, foetus and nursed infants
- Expected benefits and the purpose of the trial; if there is no clinical objective expected the participant has to know as well
- Alternative treatments for the participant and their side effects
- Compensation and insurances for the participant if he/she is harmed
- Expense allowance and possible personal expenses for the participant
- Voluntary participation and possibilities for refusal at any time (without any disadvantages for participant who dropped out)
- Open access for responsible monitors, auditors, Ethics Committees, health authorities to every medical document regarding the trial including original documents
- Data protection, especially the personal data of the patients, has to be considered
- Preservation of anonymization; documents which identify the participants have to be treated confidentially
- Update of changes of the trial for patients
- Contact person or institutions in case of harm
- Circumstances and reasons that can stop the participation or study
- Expected duration
- Approximate number of participants

Considerations to Ensure Compliance to GCP

The Ethics Committee must approve the Informed Consent Form. The form has to be translated in the patient's first language (if available), must be easy to understand and should include the current date of creation.

see 14
Ethics

After approval, the sponsor-investigator is allowed to provide the form to the participant. If the patient is under age, mentally retarded or not able to understand and sign the document autonomously, the consent process has to follow the requirements as defined in local law. In all cases, participants receive a copy of the signed form.

Advice – Hints and Tips

- Minors have to be treated with caution. They need more detailed and separate information according to their age.
- The patients should get time to collect information about the clinical trial and their questions have to be answered detailed and to their full satisfaction.
- Neither the sponsor-investigator nor any of his/her employees may influence or force a patient to participate in the study.
- The pages of the Informed Consent Form should be numbered.
- The Ethics Committee usually offers form templates!

Forms and Templates

⟳ Informed Consent Checklist
⟳ Example Informed Consent
(http://www.who.int/rpc/research_ethics/InformedConsent-clinicalstudies.doc; accessed January 11, 2011)

During Study

During the study, it is imperative that the content of the Informed Consent complies with the study or, rather, the IB. Only in this manner is the sponsor-investigator protected against any legal ramifications.

Regulatory Reference

! ICH GCP Guideline, 4.8
! EU Directive 2001/20/EC, Art. 2, Art. 3, Art. 4, Art. 5, Art. 6

Responsibilities

Participant Withdraws the Informed Consent

The patient has the right to withdraw his consent and participation in the clinical trial at any time, without indicating the reason(s) and without the danger to affect his medical care in the future.

The patient is provided a final medical examination to exclude possible side effects associated with the study. This exam constitutes the official completion date for the withdrawn patient.

Amendments during the Study

Often, there are amendments that concern the participant and/or the Informed Consent Form. Any supplement must be included in this document immediately. It is very important to note the current version number on the Informed Consent Form after any change made.

With each change, the sponsor-investigator needs to clarify to the patient again about the new Informed Consent and the participant must reconfirm his/her consent with his signature. A copy of the amended signed informed consent with the correct version number must be given to the participant.

Advice – Hints and Tips

- Every amendment to the Informed Consent Form must be delivered to the Ethics Committee for approval.
- Consider having a statement in the Informed Consent that allows all data collected up to the date of withdrawal to be analyzed, should the participant withdraw consent at any time during the study. With this statement, you can prevent the needless loss of data.

see 14
Ethics

After Study

After the completion of a clinical trial, the Informed Consent Form is still a very important document. If it has at all times reflected the regulations and the IB, then the sponsor-investigator should not have any legal issues.

Regulatory Reference

! ICH GCP Guideline, 4.8
! EU Directive 2001/20/EC, Art. 2, Art. 3, Art. 4, Art. 5, Art. 6

Responsibilities

Archiving

It is recommended to archive all the signed Informed Consent Forms for 15 years after trial completion (or cancellation).

see 15
Trial Master File,
Updating and
Archiving

The forms must be stored together with the other clinical trial documents.

According to Article 2(g) of Directive 2001/20/EC, the Investigator's Brochure (IB) is 'a compilation of the clinical and non-clinical data on the investigational medicinal product or products which are relevant to the study of the product or products in human subjects'. The Summary of Product Characteristics (SmPC) is the equivalent document for marketed products.

Regulatory Reference

! ICH GCP Guideline, Chapter 7
! EU Directive 2001/20/EC, Art. 2.7

Responsibilities

Any request for trial authorisation has to include an IB or a similar document used in place of the IB. For currently marketed products, the approved SmPC may be such a document. However, if the trial product or IMP is used not according to the approved market authorisation, the SmPC needs to be extended with a summary of all relevant clinical and non-clinical data that justifies the use of the IMP in the clinical trial. If there is no SmPC, a new IB specific to the use or indication may have to be prepared.

Availability of the IB
The sponsor-investigator should be able to retrieve the IB or an equivalent document from the commercial manufacturer of the IMP.

International Trial
If the trial is conducted in different countries and the SmPCs in the countries differ, the sponsor-investigator needs to choose one SmPC for all countries.

Example
Table of Contents of Investigator's Brochure
Confidentiality Statement (optional)
Signature Page (optional)
1 Table of Contents
2 Summary
3 Introduction
4 Physical, Chemical, and Pharmaceutical Properties and Formulation
5 Nonclinical Studies
    5.1 Nonclinical Pharmacology
    5.2 Pharmacokinetics and Product Metabolism in Animals
    5.3 Toxicology
6 Effects in Humans
    6.1 Pharmacokinetics and Product Metabolism in Humans
    6.2 Safety and Efficacy
    6.3 Marketing Experience
7 Summary of Data and Guidance for the Investigator

(Required material to be placed at the end of document)

1. Publications

    Provide legible copies of all the actual references from each section. **NB:** The reference listing corresponding to in-text citations should be found at the end of each section.

2. Reports

Appendices (if any)

Generally, the sponsor reviews the IB at least annually; however, revision to the document may have to be done more frequently if new relevant data is generated.

Investigator-initiated trials are different in this manner, since it is most often the case the sponsor-investigator is not the one providing the revised IB.

Regulatory Reference

!   ICH GCP Guideline, Chapter 7
!   EU Directive 2001/20/EC, Art. 2.7

Responsibilities

Even if revising the IB does not belong to the duties of the sponsor-investigator, according to the GCP, any relevant new information may be so important that the manufacturer should be notified. Depending on the new data, it may even have to be communicated to the IEC and/or the regulatory authorities before the new revised IB is released.

A new revised IB provided by the manufacturer needs to be forwarded to the IEC and/or the regulatory authorities concerned as soon as possible.

Advice – Hints and Tips

Even if a revised IB is available, all older versions of the IB need to be archived.

Running a clinical trial would be impossible without an adequate insurance protection. The sponsor-investigator, the clinical trial staff as well as the trial subjects must be insured, with the Ethics Committee approving the complete insurance coverage. After the Ethics Committee gives a positive vote, the clinical trial can start.

Regulatory Reference

! ICH GCP Guideline, Chapter 5.8
! EU Directive 2001/20/EC, Art. 3.2(f) and 6.3(i)

Responsibilities

There must be an insurance policy for the trial participants and the sponsor-investigator.

Trial Participants

The trial participants have to be insured in case of death, permanent or temporary illness. The insurance sum by law is approximately 500,000 Euro per participant.

Trial participants' insurance contains an accident-, liability-, personal- and indemnity-insurance. It is called 'sui generis'.

see 14
Ethics

In addition to the above-mentioned insurances, the Ethics Committee requires home-to-clinic accident insurance.

Sponsor-Investigator

The sponsor-investigator normally is protected by his own insurance against all legal and financial claims. However, he is not protected in any case of medical malpractice or negligence in the conduct of a clinical trial.

The insurance company should be informed about:

- The name of the study
- The reason for the study
- Time period of the study
- Number of participants
- Claim of insurance and extent of coverage
- The sponsor-investigators/sub-investigators and clinical centre(s)

Advice – Hints and Tips

For clinical trials, all respective legal requirements regarding any insurance should be considered. The sponsor-investigator has to know:

- What kind of insurance is required?
- Is it necessary to insure the medical trial staff as well?
- Is it possible to get compensation for pain and suffering?
- How much is the limit of indemnity for the insurance policy?

The insured sum depends on the risk assessment, the duration and the number of participants.

During the clinical trial, communication between the sponsor-investigator and the insurance company is usually not necessary. Nevertheless, a few circumstances warrant adequate communication and reporting.

Regulatory Reference

! ICH GCP Guideline, Chapter 8.2.5

Responsibilities

Sponsor-Investigator

The sponsor-investigator is responsible for checking that the insurance is current and valid. He/she must approach the insurance company in the case of:

- The recruitment period is extended and an extension of the insurance period is required
- General extension or termination of the study
- Changes to the number of participants, the length of treatment and/or additional measures
- New trial sites or new clinical trial staff additions

All changes in relation to the insurance company must also be reported to the Ethics Committee.

The national health authorities work to ensure adherence to the local regulations and legislation; clinical trials can only begin with their permission. They also work with the sponsor-investigator to ensure patients or participants are not exposed to excessive risks or harm. The following chapter reviews all requirements implemented according to the ICH GCP and the European Directives.

Regulatory Reference

!   ICH GCP Guideline, Chapters 5.10, 8
!   EU Directive 2001/20/EC, Art. 9
!   Detailed guidance for the request for authorisation of a clinical trial on a medicinal product for human use to the competent authorities, notification of substantial amendments and declaration of the end of the trial, chapter 4.1

Responsibilities

Limitations
The clinical trial cannot start until the sponsor-investigator has implemented in the study planning all the requirements prescribed by the national regulations, and the health authority has approved the application for study initiation.

!   Bear in mind that this chapter only describes the requirements of the ICH-GCP and the European Directives, which were implemented in most national regulations. It is possible that the local health authority will have additional requirements for the study, which must be considered.
!   In addition, this chapter only reviews the standard application procedure for obtaining clinical trial authorization i.e. without special circumstances. Special conditions and regulations regarding IMPs, the Study Protocol and IB/SmPC are explained in the relevant chapters.

Normally, the sponsor-investigator receives a EudraCT number for the study's entry into the EudraCT database **before** submitting the Clinical Trial Application (CTA) to the health authority for approval.

see 8
EudraCT

Clinical Trial Application (CTA)
The first step is to compile a submission package including a formal application with a covering letter and all the essential documents mentioned below. Up-to-date request forms and procedures are available on the EudraCT database website. Compile your CTA based on their website. The instructions for finding CTA forms are described in the chapter, EudraCT.

A covering letter must include:

•   The EudraCT number
•   The Study Protocol number
•   The title of the clinical trial

The covering letter should address any important issues, such as unusual study design, special population groups or IMPs. The covering letter text should also mention where these objectives are listed within the application. Any recommendations or advice documents obtained from the EMA, the national authorities or the member state should be taken into consideration. Again, references should be made to where these documents can be found in the application.

The submission package should be submitted to the responsible health authority after you have received the EudraCT number and registered the trial on the EudraCT database. The sponsor-investigator must date every submission or resubmission. Each submission must have a unique relation to a Study Protocol. For multicentre clinical trials, submissions have to be made to the health authorities in every concerned Member State where the study is to be conducted.

Deficiency Letters

It is possible that the health authority raises objections with regard to your application. If this happens, you will receive a Deficiency Letter from the authority. This correspondence has to be dated. This Deficiency Letter provides the sponsor-investigator **only one further opportunity** to submit an improved application. If the application is not changed in accordance with the requirements mentioned in the Deficiency Letter, it will be refused. The study cannot begin and you must create an entirely new submission package.

Timelines

The application has to be answered within **60 days** of submission by the responsible health authority. Local national laws can regulate this period to less than 60 days, but not more. The health authority can send a notification that there is no reason for disagreement before the due date elapses.

Approval of Clinical Trial Application

If the sponsor-investigator receives an approval letter from the health authority, it is assumed the submission (or resubmission) is approved. The approval, called the Clinical Trial Authorisation, is only effective for one clinical trial and member state.
If one of the following occurs, the health authority may withdraw or suspend the approval.

- Important conditions are violated
- You do not submit important changes and amendments within the due dates

Essential Documents and Requirements

The submission packages/applications must contain the following essential documents. In doing so, you will meet the minimum requirements for document harmonization and conform to GCP and its implementation in the national legislation. Under certain circumstances, you can combine some of these documents. It may be enough to submit only a copy of the documents (e.g. for multicentre trials).

- IB/SmPC
- Study protocol and amendments
- CRF
- Informed Consent Form (patient information and advertisements)
- Financing
- Insurance

see 15
Trial Master File, Updating and Archiving

- Contracts
- Ethics
- Qualifications, CVs of site staff, training, delegation of authority
- Scheduled medical and technical tests
    - Certificates and validations
    - Approvals of authorities
    - Internal and external quality controls
- Normal values of scheduled tests
- Treatment of IMP (per GMP)/used materials
- Shipping documents for IMP and materials
- Decoding procedure for blinding studies
- Pre-study monitor report

Before submitting the documents, you should check if all the requirements for each document have been met in your application (CTA) for the relevant health authority (country- or region-specific).

The corresponding chapter headings provide further information on these documents.

In this chapter's section 'Forms and Templates', a detailed overview of the requirements for different countries in the European Area ('Information required by Member States for applications to a competent authority') is provided.

Advice – Hints and Tips

- Bear in mind that the best chance for health authority approval happens when all procedures and documentation conform to GCP, GLP and GMP.
- Submissions and amendments should be submitted in the language required and provided by the national health authority.
- Ensure that all relevant Ethics Committee(s) agree with the plan and the project.
- Bear in mind that you must notify the health authorities about all substantial amendments to the Study Protocol.

see 14
Ethics

Health Authorities
Further information about any additional requirements given by local law can be found on the website of the responsible health authority. Addresses (URLs) of authorities in the European Area are provided at the end of the book.

Forms and Templates

◡ 'Information required by MS for applications to a competent authority': Requirements_CA.pdf
(excerpt from 2005 full document: http://ec.europa.eu/health/files/eudralex/vol-10/11_ca_14-2005_en.pdf)

During Study

Operational Instructions

- Follow the instructions on the EudraCT database to complete the CTA

Clinical trials commence only after most of the health authority-related issues have been resolved. But what should be done if there are any changes made in the study? What should be done if there are additions to the Study Protocol? It is also your responsibility to notify the health authorities and obtain approval from them during the trial. Failure to do so might result in the withdrawal of the Clinical Trial Authorisation.

Regulatory Reference

! EU Directive 2001/20/EC, Art. 10 a
! Detailed guidance for request for authorisation of a clinical trial on a medicinal product for human use to the competent authorities, notification of substantial amendments and declaration of the end of a trial, chapter 4.2

Responsibilities

Amendments
Amendments are supplements or changes to any part or any parameters of a clinical trial. They can be related to the trial procedures, to the conducting of the study, to the Study Protocol, to the IMP, to the safety of patients/participants or to the clinical documents. One amendment could refer to several changes and supplements in the Study Protocol or the clinical documents.

1. Substantial Amendments
An amendment is always substantial if it will have a significant impact on any of the following:

see 14
Ethics

- **The safety or physical or mental integrity of the subjects**
- **The scientific value of the trial**
- **The conduct or management of the trial**
- **The quality or safety of any IMP used in the trial**

The competent authority and/or Ethics Committee(s) must be notified about any substantial amendments. Check your local requirements and consult the chapter, 'Ethics' to learn who has to be notified regarding an amendment.

Even if only one body has to be notified, you should also send a notification to the other; this means you should send a similar notification 'for information only'. You should not have to expect a decision or an approval from the second 'informational notification'. However, if both parties require notification, be sure to submit in parallel.

A substantial amendment should include:

- A covering letter, explaining why the amendment should be considered as substantial
- An application form, which
    - identifies the clinical trial (title, EudraCT number, sponsor's protocol code number)
    - identifies the applicant
    - identifies the amendment (sponsor's amendment number and date)
    - describes the amendment and why it is necessary
- An extract of the modified documents, showing previous and new wording, if applicable
- The new version of the modified documents, particularly when the changes are so widespread and/or substantial that they justify a new version, identified with updated version number and date
- Supporting information (if applicable)
    - Summaries of data
    - An updated overall risk-benefit assessment
    - Possible consequences for subjects already included in the trial
    - Possible consequences for the evaluation of the results
- Where applicable, if a substantial amendment changes the core data or the full application form data set (according to national requirements) in the XML file that accompanied the initial application for the trial, the sponsor-investigator should submit a revised copy of the XML file with the Notification of Amendment, incorporating the amended data. The application for substantial amendment should identify the fields to be changed, by attaching a printout of the revised form showing the amended fields highlighted

Use the form 'Notification of a substantial amendment to a clinical trial on a medicinal product for human use to the competent authorities and for opinion of the Ethics Committees in the Community' provided in the this chapter's section 'Forms and Templates'.

2. Non-Substantial Amendments
Non-substantial amendments are all other amendments that do not pertain to the four criteria of a substantial amendment mentioned above. The responsible health authority and/or Ethics Committees do not have to be notified of non-substantial amendments and can be implemented without hesitation.

3. Urgent Amendments
This type of amendment is exceptional. The sponsor-investigator can take measures immediately without prior authorisation of the competent authority if safety and health of the trial subjects are directly threatened and in danger.

In the majority of these cases, such a measure is the immediate (temporary) stop of the trial. The sponsor-investigator must notify the competent authority and Ethics Committees as soon as possible, e.g. by telephone at first, about the event which occurred, the measures taken by the sponsor-investigator and the proposed next steps. When the safety and health of the trial participants are secured against the critical incident, the sponsor-investigator must submit a substantial amendment.

Review this chapter's section 'After Study', for more details regarding temporary interruptions in a trial.

Kinds of Changes and Supplements

A substantial amendment is one that must be submitted and notified only if you identified a change that belongs to one of the following aspects mentioned below and the change has significant impact to the criteria of a substantial amendment. Otherwise, the changes can be notified as non-substantial amendment.

1. Study Protocol

Changes in any of the following would be considered substantial amendments:

- Purpose of trial
- Design of trial
- Informed consent
- Recruitment procedure
- Measures of efficacy
- Schedule of samples
- Addition or deletion of tests or measures
- Number of participants
- Age range of participants
- Inclusion criteria
- Exclusion criteria
- Safety monitoring
- Duration of exposure to the IMP(s)
- Change of posology of the IMP(s)
- Change of comparator
- Statistical analysis

Examples:
- A reduction in the number of clinic visits might impact on the safety or physical or mental integrity of the subjects.
- Introducing a new monitoring procedure or a change in the principal investigator might significantly affect the conduct or the management of the trial, respectively.
- The use of a new measurement for the primary endpoint could alter the scientific value of the trial.
- Altering the procedure for IMP reconstitution and administration could affect the safe use of an IMP in the trial.

2. Clinical Trial Authorisation and its Documents

The sponsor should notify with a substantial amendment to the scientific documents submitted to support the request for a Clinical Trial Authorisation when certain new information becomes available – e.g. data from additional studies of pharmacology, toxicology or a new clinical use of the study's IMP – information which might alter the initial risk-to-benefit evaluation of the supporting documents, or any change to the IB which alters the product safety profile in such a way that the pharmacovigilance reporting will be altered.

3. Clinical Trial Application (CTA)

Some key information fitting the criteria of a substantial amendment may be documented only in the CTA form, e.g. a change to the legal representative of the sponsor in the European Community; the revocation, suspension or relevant substantial amendment of the Marketing Authorisation of the IMP; or transfer of sponsor responsibilities to a new individual or organization. Any changes to these types of key information in the CTA form should be notified as a substantial amendment.

4. Trial Arrangements
The following are usually described in the Study Protocol:

- Change of the principal investigator or the addition of new investigators
- Change of the coordinating investigator
- Change of the trial site or the addition of new sites
- Change of the sponsor or its legal representative
- Change of the CRO-assigned significant tasks
- Change of the definition of the end of the trial

5. Investigational Medicinal Product (IMP)
Any changes to the IMP's quality data, concerning:

- Name or code of IMPs
- Immediate packaging material
- Manufacturer(s) of active substance
- Manufacturing process of the active substance
- Specifications of active substance
- Manufacture of the IMP
- Specification of the IMP
- Specification of excipients, where these may affect product performance
- Shelf-life, including after first opening and reconstitution
- Major change to the formulation
- Storage conditions
- Test procedures of active substance
- Test procedures of the medicinal product
- Test procedures of non-pharmacopoeial excipients

Timelines and Implementation
Non-substantial amendments do not require notification. The sponsor-investigator can implement these amendments immediately.

The Ethic Committee(s) and the responsible health authority must decide within a pre-defined period about the validity of your substantial amendments. When an affirmative decision is received, the changes can be implemented; otherwise, the amendment must be altered or re-worded. Retry the notification with added validation or documentation to get an affirmative decision.

It is possible that you do not receive a response from the health authority. In this case, you should ask the health authority directly. The health authority can give no prior objections to the amendment or it can extend the predefined period.

In the case of an occurrence of a special event after implementation of the corrective measures given in the substantial amendment, the responsible authority and Ethics Committee(s) must be notified within **15 days** (see also 'Urgent Amendments').

Advice – Hints and Tips

Mark carefully whether you create a substantial amendment or a non-substantial amendment. Bear in mind that any change, case and/or situation are unique, thus, you must decide on a case-by-case basis. If there are any changes regarding the IMP used in your study, notify the IMP's company, which should inform all the other studies using the same IMP.

Applicants should be aware that these procedures are set out to provide the rapid and efficient processing of substantial amendments. Failing to follow the procedural aspects is one reason why unsatisfactory documentation is likely to lead to a refusal of the amendment.

Forms and Templates

○ 'Notification of a substantial amendment to a clinical trial on a medicinal product for human use to the competent authorities and for opinion of the Ethics Committees in the Community': Substantial_Amendments_Form.pdf
(http://ec.europa.eu/health/documents/eudralex/vol-10/; accessed January 11, 2011)

Operational Instructions

- Complete the form for amendments with as much detail as possible and submit it to the health authority and/or Ethics Committee(s).
- All notifications, amendments and correspondence with the authorities should be dated, copied, sorted and put in the TMF.

After finishing a clinical trial, there are still considerable requirements given by the Competent Authority. It has to be ensured that the trial was in accordance with GCP, GMP, all related directives, the local law and the Study Protocol. The health authority has the right to conduct inspections during your study in order to identify any inconsistencies with GCP or the Study Protocol. The following helps the sponsor-investigator to understand how the end of a clinical trial is defined and which measures should be taken to finish the study lawfully.

Regulatory Reference

! ICH GCP Guideline, Chapters 4.13, 5.21, 5.22
! EU Directive 2001/20/EC, Art. 10 c
! Detailed guidance for request for authorisation of a clinical trial on a medicinal product for human use to the competent authorities, notification of substantial amendments and declaration of the end of a trial, chapter 4.3

Responsibilities

How Is the End of a Clinical Trial Defined?

The completion date for the end of the study should be defined in the Study Protocol. Ensure that any changes made to this definition are notified as a **substantial amendment**.

Usually, the end of the trial is identified as the point when the last participant underwent all procedures of the trial. Deviations to this definition have to be mentioned and substantiated in the Study Protocol.

Bear in mind that there may be various trial completion dates for multicentre studies. The trial can be finished in one concerned Member State, while another one still is conducting the study. On the other hand, the study is considered finished as soon as all concerned Member States conducted the trial completely.

Premature End, Temporary Interruptions and Gaps

If the trial is terminated earlier than planned or the study is interrupted for whatever reason, a notification to the responsible health authority in the concerned Member State must be submitted. In addition, the authority demands further explanation about the reasons and circumstances for premature end or temporary stops. The notification can be sent, in the case of a halt, as a substantial amendment, and, in case of premature end, as a declaration of end. When there is a temporary stop, send a similar notification to the Ethics Committee(s).

Use the forms:

- 'Notification of a substantial amendment to a clinical trial on a medicinal product for human use to the competent authorities and for opinion of the Ethics Committees in the Community' for interruption of the trial or
- 'Notification of the End of a Clinical Trial of a Medicine for Human Use to the Competent Authority and the Ethics Committee' for termination of the trial

found in this chapter's section 'Forms and Templates'.

The above-mentioned procedure is used both when the termination or interruption is initiated by the sponsor-investigator and when the sponsor-investigator receives a suspension from the health authorities.

In order to recommence a temporarily interrupted trial, the sponsor-investigator must submit a request to the authority as a further substantial amendment. The sponsor-investigator and the request justification must verify that a restart will be safe and harmless. For the request of restart, the same form may be used as that for the interruption.

If the decision is made to not recommence with the study, proceed as if there is a premature end of the study.

Scheduled End

Even if the study ends as scheduled without special circumstances, the sponsor-investigator must send the notification for the end of the clinical trial to each health authority in all concerned Member States where the trial was conducted.

Use the form, 'Notification of the End of a Clinical Trial of a Medicine for Human Use to the Competent Authority and the Ethics Committee' in this chapter's section 'Forms and Templates'.

Content of Notification

If the provided template for notification of the end of the clinical trial is not used, remember that the following points are required:

- Name and address of the sponsor or his legal representative in the Member State
- Title of the trial
- EudraCT number
- Sponsor-investigator's protocol code number
- Date of end of trial in the concerned Member State
- Date of end of complete trial in all participating centres in all countries, if available

After Termination

Whenever a trial is terminated, the local authorities require a summary of the Final Study Report, irrespective of whether or not the study ends as scheduled or unscheduled.

see 26
Final Study Report and
Publication

For the summary of the Final Study Report, use the form 'Synopsis for Clinical Trial Report' in this chapter's section, 'Forms and Templates'. This report summary should be in accordance as well with local regulatory requirements as with GCP. If the authorities demand more documents than the summary, such as the whole Final Study Report or other essential documents, the mentioned documents with the required level of detail must be submitted.

The Final Study Report should, at a minimum, provide the following information when the study has a premature end:

- Justification of the premature ending or of the temporary halt of the trial
- Number of patients still receiving treatment at time of study termination
- Proposed management of patients receiving treatment at time of halt or study termination
- Consequences for the evaluation of study results

Furthermore, the responsible authorities have to enter the termination information into the EudraCT database. This means that the trial is formally closed.

see 8
EudraCT

Special events such as adverse events may occur after the termination of the trial. If this occurs and if it seems to have a significant impact on the benefit and risk analysis, or in any way impact the participant's health, the sponsor-investigator must notify all concerned health authorities and Ethics Committees. He/she must also provide what will be the proposed next steps.

see 1
Risk-Benefit Analysis

Timelines

The notification should be sent within **90 days** after finishing the study to the authorities, in the case the trial ends as scheduled. If the trial ends earlier, then the notification should be within **15 days**. Substantial amendments for interruption and possibility for resuming have to be sent within **15 days**. The summary of the Clinical Trial Report has to be sent within **1 year** after finishing.

Advice – Hints and Tips

Try to submit notifications and amendments as soon and with as much detail as possible. This will save time, prevent delayed deliveries and avoid unnecessary requests. Delays and incomplete or incorrect information might incur hard sanctions or other radical measures taken by the authorities. Make sure all documents that are relevant for the authorities are archived correctly after the termination of the study and have a source to the information for later requests.

Decide carefully whether the study needs to be stopped temporarily or terminated completely. Always keep in mind the protection of the patient's health and a positive benefit and risk analysis are more important than any economic and/or financial disadvantages.

Each country's responsible authorities may have their own forms and templates. Check with them beforehand; the relevant websites are listed at the end of the book.

Forms and Templates

- 'Notification of a substantial amendment to a clinical trial on a medicinal product for human use to the competent authorities and for opinion of the Ethics Committees in the Community': Substantial_Amendments_Form.pdf (http://ec.europa.eu/health/documents/eudralex/vol-10/; accessed January 11, 2011)
- 'Notification of the End of a Clinical Trial of a Medicine for Human Use to the Competent Authority and the Ethics Committee': Declaration_Of_The_End_Of_Trial.pdf (http://ec.europa.eu/health/documents/eudralex/vol-10/; accessed January 11, 2011)
- 'Synopsis for Final Study Report': Synopsis_Form.pdf (excerpt from www.ema.europa.eu/ema/pages/includes/document/open_document. jsp?webContentId=WC500002832)

Operational Instructions

- Compile your submissions in accordance to the mentioned requirements (complete the forms as much as possible).
- It is very important to send your amendments, notifications and summary of the Final Study Report within the due dates to the regulatory authorities.
- All notifications, amendments and correspondence with the authorities should be copied, sorted and placed in the TMF.

To carry out a clinical trial, the fundamentals of ethics must be strictly in compliance. An independent Ethics Committee (IEC) at the study site controls these adherences. The IEC is a consortium of physicians, scientists and non-medical members from the study site or local community. Their responsibilities are to protect the rights, the safety and the well-being of all clinical trial participants at their institution.

Before the implementation of a clinical trial, the IEC has to give a favourable vote; otherwise, the trial cannot begin.

Clinical trials should be conducted in accordance with the ethical principles that have their origin in the Declaration of Helsinki and be consistent with GCP and the applicable regulatory requirement(s).

Regulatory Reference

! ICH GCP Guideline, Chapters 3, 4.4
! Declaration of Helsinki
! EU Directive 2001/20/EC, Art. 3.2(a), Art. 6

Responsibilities

Required Documents
To get a positive vote from the IEC, submit the following documents:

- Trial protocol(s)/amendment(s)
- Written informed consent form(s) and consent from updates
- Subject recruitment procedures (e.g. advertisement)
- Written information to be provided to participants
- The IB, if available
- Available safety information
- Information about payments and compensation available to participants
- The sponsor-investigator's current curriculum vitae and/or other documentation evidencing qualifications
- The suitability of the sponsor-investigator and supporting staff
- The quality of the facilities
- The adequacy and completeness of the written information to be given and the procedure to be followed for the purpose of obtaining informed consent and the justification for the research on persons incapable of giving informed consent as regards the specific restrictions laid down in Article 3 of the EU Directive 2001/20/EC
- Provision for indemnity or compensation in the event of injury or death attributable to a clinical trial
- Any insurance or indemnity to cover the liability of the sponsor-investigator
- The amounts and, where appropriate, the arrangements for rewarding or compensating sponsor-investigator's and trial participants and the relevant aspects of any agreement between the sponsor-investigator and the trial site
- The arrangement for the recruitment of participants
- Any other documents that the IEC may need to fulfil its responsibilities

see 11
Investigator's
Brochure/Summary
of Product
Characteristics

Responsibilities of the Independent Ethics Committee (IEC)

As the IEC is responsible for the protection of the rights, the safety and the well-being of the trial participants, all documents will be put to the 'acid test'. A clinical trial may be initiated only if the IEC and/or the competent authority come to the conclusion that the anticipated therapeutic and public health benefits justify the risks and may be continued only if compliance with this requirement is permanently monitored.

The sponsor-investigator should know that the IEC is required to monitor or control the trial at regular intervals to ensure that there is an appropriate benefit/risk for the trial participants.

The IEC can demand that the sponsor-investigator must deliver more information to the trial participants if any new information advances the rights, the safety and/or the well-being of the trial participants substantially.

This committee also would review any disbursement amounts and method of payment to avoid that the payment serves as an enticement.

see 10
Informed Consent

This information has to be written down in the Informed Consent.

Respites of the Evaluation/Application

Within **60 days** from the date of the receipt, the IEC is required to decide whether a favourable vote can be given and the study can be authorized to start.

If medical products for gene therapy or somatic therapy, or medical products containing genetically modified organisms are tested, an extension of **30 days** is permitted.

Furthermore, the authorization period can be **extended another 90 days** in the event of a consultation of a group or a committee in accordance with regulations and procedures of the Member States.

In the case of xenogenic cell therapy, there are no time limits to the authorization period.

The Member States are allowed to shorten the 60-day period on their own. If the sponsor-investigator has any amendments, the IEC has **35 days** from the date of the receipt of the proposed amendments to give an opinion.

Advice – Hints and Tips

- The Informed Consent of trial participants should be revised when important new information becomes available. All revisions to the Informed Consent Form and any written information provided to the study participants should also receive the IEC's favourable opinion in advance of use. The trial participants should be informed as quickly as possible.
- The protection of the trial participants have to be justified by reference to the toxicological investigations before the trial starts.

The International Code of Medical Ethics declares that, 'A physician shall act in the patient's best interest when providing medical care'.

According to this declaration, the sponsor-investigator has to ensure that during the trial, any necessary amendment to the protocol is made and that the rights, the safety and the well-being of all trial participants are protected at all times.

Regulatory Reference

! ICH GCP Guideline, Chapters 4.11, 4.12, 4.4.2, 4.4.3, 5.11, 5.17.1, 5.21
! Declaration of Helsinki
! EU Directive 2001/20/EC, Art. 6, Art. 9, Art. 10.1, Art. 10.2, Art. 16.3, Art. 17

Responsibilities

Amendment to the Study Protocol

If there are significant or substantial amendments, which refer to the safety of the trial participants or can change the interpretation of the scientific documents in support of the conduct of the trial or are substantial in any other way, the sponsor-investigator should inform the competent authorities and the IEC concerning the reasons for and content of these amendments in accordance with Articles 6 and 9 of the EU Directive 2001/20/EC.

After receiving the suggested change, the IEC has to approve the amendments according to the rights, the safety and the well-being of the trial participants. The IEC should give a statement within **35 days** after receipt.

In case of an unfavourable statement, the sponsor-investigator is not allowed to change the protocol; he/she may attempt to re-apply for an amendment until successful, however, this may affect the timelines of the study.

If the statement is positive and none of the competent authorities has doubts regarding the amendments, the sponsor-investigator is able to continue the trial after the adaption of the proposed amendment to the protocol.

AEs, SAEs and SUSARs

In case of death of a trial participant, the sponsor-investigator is required to notify the IEC and should provide additional information.

The sponsor-investigator must care that all important information about SAEs and SUSARs, which could lead to or where leading to death, should be documented and redirected to the competent authorities and the IEC as quickly as possible, **7 days** at most, after the sponsor-investigator is aware of the event. Subsequently, the sponsor-investigator has **8 days** to submit any missing information.

see 11
Investigator's
Brochure/Summary
of Product
Characteristics

All other SAEs and SUSARs should be referred to the competent authorities and the IEC as soon as possible, **15 days at most**, after the time of occurrence.

Once a year during the conduct of the trial, the sponsor-investigator must submit a list/schedule of all SAEs and SUSARs that have occurred during the trial to the competent authorities and the IEC. At a minimum, the sponsor-investigator must produce a report about all the trial participants' safety.

After Study

After a study is closed, the authors, editors and publishers have ethical obligations with regard to the publication of the results of the research.

Regulatory Reference

- ! ICH GCP Guideline, Chapter 4.13
- ! Declaration of Helsinki
- ! EU Directive 2001/20/EC, Art. 10.3
- ! EU Directive 2005/28/EC, Chapter 2, Art. 6.2

Responsibilities

see 8
EudraCT

Within 90 days after the end of the trial, the sponsor-investigator should inform the competent authorities and the IEC that the trial is completed.

In the case of an early termination, the sponsor-investigator has only 15 days to inform the competent authorities and the IEC, and must also explain the reasons for termination.

Advice – Hints and Tips

Please note: after a study has ended, the IEC is required to store the essential documents of all clinical trials for a period of at least 3 years. If there are special requirements, they have to store the documents according to their own standard operating procedures.

Before Initiation

In *investigator-initiated trials* (also called *non-commercial trials*), the sponsor-investigator usually establishes only one file for collecting all study documents. This is in contrast to *commercial trials*, where two files are maintained appropriate for the investigator and the sponsor.

The *Trial Master File* (TMF) is the record for documentation and archiving of all accumulated study documents, particularly with regard to the *essential documents* for conducting clinical trials.

Regulatory Reference

- ! ICH GCP Guideline, section 8.2
- ! EU Directive 2001/20/EC, Art. 15.5
- ! EU Directive 2005/28/EC, section 4, Art. 16

*[handwritten: lookup ... * Fridam 27rd.]*

Responsibilities

Purpose

[handwritten: ACADIA-kal]

At the beginning of the trial, the *sponsor-investigator* and the *monitor* (if applicable, particularly in the case of multicentre trials) are responsible for the documents stored in the TMF. Correct handling ensures evidence of conformity with GCP.

On the other hand, careless handling of trial documents and the TMF can interfere with the validity of the clinical trial and the quality and reliability of the obtained data. Thus, a careful organization and handling in the TMF is quite important, particularly when the data may be inspected by the health authority or other competent authorities. In case of such an inspection, these third parties require direct access to the participants' study documents, but not before the patients have given written consent.

see 10
Informed Consent

Essential Documents

The list given below is according to ICH GCP and represents the essential documents needed before the clinical phase of the trial starts:

[handwritten left margin: IB = Investigator Brochure.]
[handwritten right: investigated medical product.]

- IB/SmPC or other specific and current information about the IMP
- Signed clinical trial protocol and amendments, as necessary, and the blank CRF design
- Informed Consent Form *[handwritten: ICF]*
- Financing statements
- Insurance statements (especially for trial-specific interventions)
- Signed contracts between the trial parties (e.g. sponsor-investigator and pharmaceutical or medicine-technical company)
- Opinion and composition of the IEC
- Any written information provided to study participants, e.g. recruitment leaflets or advertising material
- Authorization/approval/notification of the protocol by the health authority in compliance with the applicable regulatory requirement(s)
- Documents regarding the qualifications (curriculum vitae, etc.) of the sponsor-investigator/subinvestigator(s) and other involved trial staff

[handwritten left margin: IEC = independent ethics committee.]

[handwritten left margin: Trial Master File TMF.]

- Normal value(s) and range(s) for medical/laboratory/technical procedures and tests as
  well as the proof of competence of the procedure and/or test
- Sample labelling for IMP container(s)
- Instructions concerning the IMP and trial-related materials (normally described in the
  Protocol or IB), in particular:
  - Handling (e.g. storage, packaging, dispensing)
  - Distribution (e.g. distribution dates and methods, batch numbers, tracking, condi-
    tion review and accountability)
- Decoding procedures for blinded trials (from third party, if applicable)
- The Master Randomization List (from third party, if applicable)
- The Pre-Trial Monitoring Report/Trial Initiation Monitoring Report, especially in case of
  multicentre trials

Examples of these essential documents can be found in the various sections and chapters
of this book or downloaded from the competent authorities.

Advice – Hints and Tips

In addition to the essential documents as defined in ICH GCP, please consider the following as important in practice to place in the TMF:

- Correspondence in each way
- Meeting minutes
- Structure of the study database
- Annotated CRF and forms, etc.

Furthermore, the sponsor-investigator should have available document folders, office
equipment and other office materials. It is necessary to prepare the register of the TMF
with a table of contents. If applicable, the sponsor-investigator can assign trial staff for
preparing the TMF.

Additional information about the content of the TMF can also be found in the EU Guidance document 'Recommendations on the Content of Trial Master File and Archiving'
from July 2006 (see this chapter's section 'Forms and Templates').

A well-organised content structure is recommended for safe and simple use of the TMF.

Forms and Templates

Examples provided:

- TMF_Table of Contents.pdf
- Recommendation2006EU_Content_TMF.pdf
  (http://ec.europa.eu/health/files/eudralex/vol-10/v10_chap5_en.pdf;
  accessed January 11, 2011)

Operational Instructions

The listed documents in Section 8 of the ICH GCP are chronologically grouped by the phase of the study in which the documents should normally be generated.

However, this grouping may not be useful for the table of contents. It is more appropriate and might be more practical, to file, for example, to have revisions, amendments or updates to documents (if applicable) together with the initial versions in the TMF, i.e. placed behind the originals using a separating sheet. This allows the sponsor-investigator or the trial staff (e.g. study nurse) to get an overview about the state of the study more easily and quickly.

During the conduct of a clinical trial, it is possible that changes with regard to contents or formal updates are required. It is not unusual that such corrections arise, particularly in an advanced phase of the study and IMP development. Changes concerning the clinical trial protocol are mostly defined as **substantial amendments** (e.g. affects the safety of the trial participant, mistaken or unclear interpretations of the scientific documents, or study-related personnel issues).

The sponsor-investigator is responsible for updating the Trial Master File (TMF) frequently. Thus, it is important to have the latest information about the progress of the clinical trial on hand. It is a fact that a TMF can rapidly consist of many volumes, although perhaps the clinical trial itself is not designed as an extensive project.

The issue of archiving the TMF should not be underestimated. To succeed, the process has to be well organized and thought out. Thus, it is important to recognize early on that archiving all essential trial-related documents will claim considerable space and time.

Regulatory Reference

! ICH GCP Guideline, sections 6.10, 6.13, 8.3
! EU Directive 2001/20/EC, section 15.5, Art. 10 a)
! EU Directive 2005/28/EC, section 4, Art. 16

Responsibilities

Revisions, Updates and Amendments

(a) Related to Regulatory Requirements

According to the regulatory requirements, it is essential that all new relevant information and documents be added immediately to the existing documents in the TMF. A well-managed update system may well guarantee the continuation of the clinical trial, particularly when there is an inspection by the competent authorities. Each version of a document has to be identified correctly with an appropriate title, the version number (if applicable) and the current date for the amendment or revision. Substantial modifications should be traceable in reference to the initial version of a document.

This includes, in particular:

- IB/ SmPC
- Clinical trial protocol/amendment(s) and the CRF  *← a Prescreening form ACAPIA study.*
- Any written information given to trial participants (Informed Consent Form, advertisements, etc.)
- Curriculum vitae of new sponsor-investigator(s)/subinvestigator(s) and supporting trial staff to whom investigator tasks are delegated

(b) Related to Ethics Committee(s) and/or Health Authorities

The Ethics Committee requires a notification, in addition to the health authority requiring a submission, when there are changes to any of listed documents above. Any competent authority approval and the additional ethical opinion are also filed in TMF. This kind of documentation is necessary to prove the compliance with the applicable regulatory requirements.

see 13
Health Authority
Approval

see 14
Ethics

(c) Related to Medical/Laboratory/Technical Procedures/Tests

If normal values or ranges are redefined during the clinical trial, it is necessary to document these changes or updates. In addition, recent proof of quality controls, accreditation of procedures, or tests conducted to ensure the adequacy of the investigation during the entire study period should be documented.

(d) Related to the Investigational Medicinal Product (IMP)

Updated information and instructions concerning the IMP and other trial-related materials must also be placed in the TMF. Furthermore, the sponsor-investigator has to document the accountability of the IMP at the study site and that the product(s) have been used according to the trial protocol.

Reports

This section includes, for example, the **Monitoring Visit Report** (in case of multicentre trials), particularly, the documentation of implausible findings by the monitor, and the interim or annual reports to the Ethics Committee and the competent authority.

Source Documents and Case Report Forms (CRF)

Regarding the source documents, all written information on the diagnosis, medical treatment and the case history of the patient should be summarized. In particular, a well-structured medical chart is imperative for a clinical trial to substantiate the integrity of the collected study data and to verify the existence of the trial participant.

see 16
Documentation

see 5
Case Report Forms

For confirming the conducted observations of the trial participant, the sponsor-investigator or an authorized member of the clinical trial staff is responsible to check whether the CRF is completed, signed and dated (per patient visit or as required). Every further change, addition or correction made to the CRF must be dated and signed by the authorized person who made the corrections and must also be endorsed by the sponsor-investigator.

For tracking entries and/or corrections on CRFs, the signatures and initials of all authorized persons should be documented on a signature sheet.

Pharmacovigilance and Study Participants

The storage of forms and reports for documentation and announcing the SAEs, SUSARs and other safety related information should be treated seriously by the sponsor-investigator. Furthermore, listings according to subject screening and enrolment, as well as identification codes, have to be included in the TMF.

Advice – Hints and Tips

If tissue samples or body fluids are to be retained as part of the study protocol, it is quite important to document their location and the identification (as applicable) in case assays have to be repeated.

In case of a multicentre trial, the coordinating sponsor-investigator should also have the permission of **direct access** to the obtained trial data from patients/participants outside his own study site. Permission can only be granted if this requirement was mentioned in the Informed Consent Form.

The CRF folders may be archived separately from the TMF, because they are used more frequently and, thus, it must be readily accessible.

Forms and Templates

⟳ TMF_Table of Contents.pdf

After Study

After completion of the clinical trial (or, in certain cases when the study is stopped prematurely), the methods for archiving and storing the TMF must be initiated by the sponsor-investigator.

Within the scope of clinical trials, methods of electronic data management are becoming more and more important. Today, essential documents are often scanned for electronic storage, particularly when there is not enough space for archiving the paper-based documents at the study site.

This section gives some suggestions about this topic that could be individually adapted to the study site(s). Ample considerations to the completion of the TMF, retention periods and requirements for storage premises, as well as requests management, are necessary.

Regulatory Reference

- ! ICH GCP Guideline, sections 4.9.4/5, 5.5.6–5.5.11, 5.6.3d, 6.13, 8
- ! EU Directive 2001/20/EC, Art. 15.5
- ! EU Directive 2001/83/EC, part 4 section B2
- ! EU Directive 2003/63/EC, annex (Module 5.2 c)
- ! EU Directive 2005/28/EC, section 4, Art. 17–20
- ! German GCP Ordinance 'GCP-Verordnung' 2004, section 4 § 13(10)

Responsibilities

Additional Essential Documents at the End of the Study

At first, the overall responsibility for the storage of the study records and the subject-related data remain with the sponsor-investigator.

Normally, however, a **record manager** from the study team is instructed to check once again if all essential documents in the TMF are complete, legible, accurate and unambiguous before it is released to storage.

After the **close-out** of the study site is completed, the following list of documents and reports also belong in the TMF:

- IMP accountability at site: forms for drug accountability
- Documentation of unused IMP destruction
- Completed subject identification code list
- Audit certificate (if available)
- Final trial close-out monitoring report (in multicentre trials)
- Treatment allocation and decoding documentation
- Final summary or synopsis report written by the sponsor-investigator to the Ethics Committee, and, where required/applicable, to the regulatory health authority (to document completion of trial)
- Clinical study report (for results and interpretation of trial)

Recommended Retention Period

It is necessary to be compliant with the appropriate legal retention period for clinical trial documents. However, in reference to the ICH GCP guideline, the stated retention time is often inconsistent and not defined clearly. Therefore, it is difficult to determine an internationally accepted period for storage of the essential trial documents.

According to the EU Directive in 2005, a period for at least 5 years after clinical trial completion is recommended, but many EU Member States expect a longer storage duration (e.g. Germany: 10 years according to the German GCP Ordinance).

The duration of 15 years is generally regarded as reasonable and practicable. Since clinical study reports and the subject identification code list must be kept for at least for 15 years by the sponsor-investigator, it is thus comprehensible to propose this retention period for all essential documents of the clinical trial.

Requirements for Premises and for Protection of the TMF

The sponsor-investigator must take adequate measures for archiving, with care to prevent that no document will be damaged by mistake or destroyed prematurely. He/she should also consider the premises for storage the TMF; particularly, it is important to have a system for controlled and authorized access.

Another issue in long-term storage of both paper-based and electronic documents is the environment; adequate precautions and checks need to be made for the room air conditioning. Special archiving institutes or companies provide normal value ranges of temperature and air humidity.

Moreover, preventive measures for fire protection, against water damage or other physical damage are recommended.

Requests and Archive Documentation

The essential records have to be indexed exactly in order to be able to retrieve information quickly. In the case that any adverse event or adverse reaction suspected to be related the study occurs after a participant has finished his/her last visit, the appropriate documents are used to assess the suspicion, and, if applicable, to organize the further steps (e.g. notifications).

Thus, archiving should comprise a well-organized archival loan service or database within the documentation to be able to query several requests. This *archive documentation* should give an overview about the current archive inventory and the record transactions.

Finally, information about the currently responsible record manager must be retained by the sponsor-investigator through the archived TMF.

Advice – Hints and Tips

- The access control should be conducted by the **record manager** and appointed representatives. They should be the only authorized people who have the competence and the keys to the archive or the file cabinets.
- Specific retention times and processes may be set forth in the study protocol.
- Convenient options to manage the archiving process are to consult the internal department for archiving at the study site, a public archive or an external company for off-site storage.
- The state-of-the-art in long-term storage is electronic archiving. Thus, it may be helpful to get current information on **OCR-Systems** or **eTMF**.

see 4
Study Protocol

Forms and Templates

↻ TMF_Table of Contents.pdf
↻ Archive_Request_Loan_Form.docx

This chapter and the previous chapters provide a supportive overview to the sponsor-investigator regarding different selected content, which may become an essential issue in before initiation and during the conduct of a trial.

According to ICH GCP, the concept 'documentation' is defined as any kind of record that describes or keeps the methods, the conduct/results, the factors influencing an intervention as well as the measures taken in a clinical trial. Records included are, for example, in written, electronic, magnetic or optical form and also indicate all the medical scans, x-rays, ECGs and other source documents from the patient chart.

The physician who would like to conduct even a simple interventional study must understand and be knowledgeable about before the study initiation, the necessity of and the specific requirements for trial documentation. Known as a sponsor-investigator, he/she has to consider that documentation is an essential process that is a part of every single step in a study and it is often much more than what is the understanding of documentation in a daily medical routine.

Regulatory Reference

! ICH GCP Guideline, sections 1.22, 4.9.1–3, 5.5.3, 6.4.9

Responsibilities

Physician as Sponsor-Investigator

The physician in a role as a sponsor-investigator must always bear in mind that he/she is responsible (with his/her signature as confirmation) for reviewing the information in all trial documents and the following actions related to the trial participant.

There is an 'unwritten rule': which means, if any planned action or assessment is done without the documentation and confirmation of the sponsor-investigator, this could be second-guessed, misinterpreted, or in the worst case, declared as a 'fraud' by the inspectors of the competent authority.

Investigator's Signature and Progress Notes

A normal signature often says nothing about the presence and the intensity of the sponsor-investigator's involvement in study visit activities or if he has simply performed a part in supervision in the medical routine (especially in case of multicentre trials).

First, to achieve a complete and timely overview of the sponsor-investigator's specific job, the confirmatory signature should always be linked with the current date (also the time, if possible), and, secondly, extensive details of the daily routine are required. Notes should be marked even when there is an uneventful routine examination over the duration the patient is enrolled in a study.

Sometimes, physicians may not want to make the extra effort to document these details; however, it becomes a very important question, when an unexpected event or an audit or an inspection occurs.

In particular, **progress notes** are a part of having accurate study documentation even if they are sometimes burdensome. Due to their importance and as a reminder, the key items are, e.g.:

- Next appointment with the participant
- Communication with other physicians (who perhaps also see the participant)
- Participant's signature for any reimbursement
- Comments on trends, adverse events, etc.

See this chapter's section 'Forms and Templates' for a checklist of progress notes.

Rubber Stamps

For a timesaving review process of patient findings, the sponsor-investigator may permit the use of rubber stamps on medical records. To allow this, supporting documentation (or additional documentation on the delegation of authority; see this chapter's section 'Forms and Templates' for an example) must be prepared that matches the stamp signature with an original signature.

see 7
Qualifications, CVs of Site Staff, Training, Delegation of Authority

CRF as Source Document

Does the ICH GCP standards require that 100% of the information recorded on a CRF be recorded in a medical record/chart first?

Not necessarily. On one hand, in the CRF, documented data should generally coincide with the original information in the patient chart, and, on the other hand, in some cases, data may be recorded directly on CRF.

If sections of the CRF are to be considered source documents, these sections or pages should be identified in the study protocol prior to study initiation. In addition, the sponsor-investigator or one authorized person of his trial team should sign and date the documents.

Advice – Hints and Tips

- If a rubber stamp is routinely used at the study site, then the rules regarding its use should be discussed with site staff prior to the trial initiation at the site.

Forms and Templates

○ Checklist-Progress_Notes.pdf

An essential part of conducting a clinical trial is the data management. The extensive requirements of data management mean that it cannot be performed solely by the sponsor-investigator.

Thus, it is strongly recommended to assign the tasks to a qualified section, such as the Biometry Department or a similar statistics and data management group at the study site, or the competent department of the pharmaceutical company that provides the IMP.

This chapter contains an overview of the operations regarding the data management and is not comprehensive.

Regulatory Reference

! ICH GCP Guideline, 5.1.1, 5.5
! EU Directive 2005/28/EC, Art. 5
! Society For Clinical Data Management: Good Clinical Data Management Practices 2009

Responsibilities

Data Management Plan

Before study initiation, a Data Management Plan has to be created. This plan is meant to regulate the handling of the obtained data in detail. Contents of the plan mostly concern:

- Incoming data (e.g. CRFs)
- Database structure
- Data entry
- Data validation
- Queries
- Coding
- Database closing
- Quality control
- Data transfer (e.g. to biometric department)
- Data import (e.g. laboratory data)

In this chapter's section 'Forms and Templates', you can find an example of a Data Management Plan.

Database Setup

For the entry and storage of data from the CRFs, a study database that is individually adapted to your study design is typically required. In addition, during the data entry, the database should be able to check on the plausibility of entries. Thus, the database setup and design must be carefully constructed.

This database needs to be validated and a description of the database structure has to be prepared. The validation should be documented in a protocol.

Before creating and entering information into the database, it must be decided and documented which trial-involved members are authorized to work with the database. Specially assigned personnel for data entry must be informed about the background information of the trial and be trained in data entry activities. Hence, it is also usually necessary to create a database entry manual.

Forms and Templates

◯ Example of a Data Management Plan

Operational Instructions

* Consult your study site or the pharmaceutical company providing the IMP about creating a database and a data management plan for your study.

Although one might at times appraise the effort of data management as exaggerated, the validity and correctness of the collected data is a key factor for the success of the trial.

Data management during a clinical trial occupies activities made on a high level. Because of the extensive requirements and the versatile possibilities of the activities concerning data management, the pharmaceutical company providing the IMP could be consulted at any time on several issues.

Regulatory Reference

! ICH GCP Guideline, 5.1.1, 5.5
! EU Directive 2005/28/EC, Art. 5
! Society For Clinical Data Management: Good Clinical Data Management Practices 2009

Responsibilities

Data Management Plan Amendments
During the trial, the Data Management Plan can be modified. Every alteration must be documented, including the reason and validity date.

Data Entry
The data entry is done by authorized and trained personnel according to the entry manual. A new input is documented in the entry log as part of the database.

Data Coding

To make the data comparable and explicit, it is expedient to code entries if possible. You can use several medical classifications (e.g. MedDRA, ICD, ATC, WHO Drug Dictionary, SNOMED). The Data Management Plan should indicate which classification and version is being used and who is in charge of the data coding.

Data Validation

The data needs to be validated regularly to ensure completeness, accuracy and plausibility. Therefore, it is expedient to create a Validation Plan.

In order to avoid reading and typing errors, one possibility is a second entry made by another person. Afterward, the double data-entry has to be compared and, if applicable, to be corrected by a third person.

Implemented in the programming, the database needs to be designed to check on plausibility automatically during the entry and provide procedures to identify missing data.

Self-Evident Corrections

Self-evident corrections are changes to data that can generally be made by authorized data management personnel without sending a query to the study site. For example, spelling errors are often adjusted as self-evident corrections. The sponsor-investigator should agree to the self-evident correction process and the permitted corrections should be described in the data management plan.

Queries

Query generation is necessary if there are discrepancies in the data or if corrections are needed that are not declared as self-evident corrections in the Data Management Plan.

see 23
Monitoring

For traceability reasons, the query is sent to the study site and the original form with the reply returns to the Data Management, while a copy of the query remains at the site.

The Monitoring supports the sponsor-investigator in handling the query.
The illustration below demonstrates the path of a query:

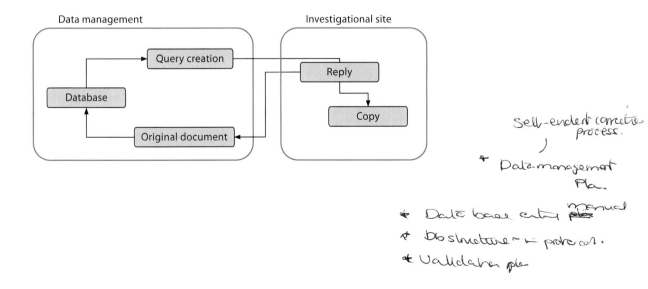

Documentation of Changes

The audit trail is a part of the database that makes it possible to reconstruct the sequence of events. Its elements should include:

- Identification of the person who made the change
- Time of change
- Explicit assignment of the subject (e.g. subject number)
- Former value, new value
- Reason for change

Advice – Hints and Tips

In data management, one should obey the rule: 'if it isn't documented, it wasn't done'. Therefore, be attentive with all parts of the documentation process, for it might protect against study failure or sloppy omission.

Sensitive trial data should be treated cautiously. Therefore, after the study, it is necessary to protect data against unauthorized changes and to ensure correct archiving.

Similar to the previous chapters on data management, this chapter only contains an overview about the activities in data management, assuming that tasks previously also have been assigned to a qualified section.

Regulatory Reference

! ICH GCP Guideline, 5.1.1, 5.5
! EU Directive 2005/28/EC, Art. 5
! Society For Clinical Data Management: Good Clinical Data Management Practices 2009

Responsibilities

Database Lock

Changes to the present data in the database are only possible when the database is locked.

When all participants (with exception to drop-outs) have completed the study, all queries are resolved and the data review is completed, the database is locked against further entries by the data management personnel. The locking process and date have to be documented.

Distributing to Biometry

After the database is locked, the data is reasonably arranged and transferred to biometry.

see 24
Biometry

Archiving

The database must be archived by the study site. The duration of data storage is defined by each national regulatory body, but at least as long as stated in the TMF.

see 15
Trial Master File, Updating and Archiving

Before Initiation

In clinical trial research, there is a distinction between a screening study and **Screening**.

While the first refers to the estimation of the accuracy and value of a screening test, **Screening** is the essential method to evaluate the patient's eligibility for participation in a clinical trial regarding the *inclusion and exclusion criteria* – according to the study protocol – and is part of the recruitment process.

Regulatory Reference

! ICH GCP Guideline, Chapter 8.3.20
! Detailed guidance on the application format and documentation to be submitted in an application for an Ethics Committee opinion on the clinical trial on medicinal products for human use, attachment 5

Responsibilities

Definition of the Recruitment-Time and -Rate

It is essential to determine the time frame and rate of recruitment to conduct the planned screening effectively.

Pre-Selection of Patients

Prior to the commencement of the trial, the sponsor-investigator should make a pre-selection of eligible patients by reviewing potential research participants, with e.g. chronic diseases (including information about health, medical history etc.), individuals who fit the appropriate inclusion criteria and contact them beforehand.

Creation of a Screening Log

In accordance with ICH GCP, the sponsor-investigator must create a **Screening Log** and document therein the identification of all research participants who take part in the pre-trial screening.

In addition, screening failures (patients which do not meet all inclusion criteria) should be specified in the Screening Log by giving reasons for the contraindication, such that the quantity of ineligible patients is replicable or perhaps some inclusion criteria could be adjusted to the patient population (this also requires changes to the protocol and CRF).

Advice – Hints and Tips

- Please note, in case of a clinical trial with patients receiving outpatient treatment you can increase your recruitment-rate by <u>additional advertising</u> in newspapers, pharmacies and medical offices, etc.
  - This advertisement must also follow strict regulations.
  - Clarify whether you approach patients in the right way.
- Ensure that your pre-selection is in accordance with the protocol.
- Because most patients do not understand medical issues or terminology, speak plainly and use straightforward words to clarify the purpose of the screening/clinical trial procedures.

Forms and Templates

- Included are two templates; a Screening Log and an Identification Register/Log that could possibly be used during the pre-selection of potential patients.

↻ Example: Subject Screening and Enrolment Log
↻ Example: Subject Identification Log

Directly after the national health authority and the local Ethics Committee have approved the study protocol and its planned conduction, and the trial initiation visit at the study site has been completed, the sponsor-investigator is allowed to begin with the recruitment and the enrolment of eligible patients, some of which maybe have been already pre-selected and listed in the Screening Log.

see 13
Health Authority Approval

Regulatory Reference

! Declaration of Helsinki
! Society for Clinical Data Management: Good Clinical Data Management Practices 2009

Responsibilities

Screening Visit and Procedures

Before any screening procedures (brief physical examinations, blood tests, etc.) are performed for the purpose of confirming the eligibility in participating in the clinical trial in an initial screening visit, the sponsor-investigator must clarify in simple, accurate and clear details to the potential participant and obtain an Informed Consent from her or him. The patient/participant must also be informed about any withdrawal period from current medication the patient is taking *(wash-out)* up to now, if such a procedure is required per the study protocol.

see 10
Informed Consent

see 14
Ethics

Generally, the Ethics Committee oversees screening procedures.

Enrolment (Run-In-Phase) and Registration of Eligible Patients

After the first subject has been enrolled in the study, the person or department designated to monitor the trial should be informed. This is recommended in order to allow for an early monitoring visit, which, in turn, can help ensure that the enrolment is in compliance with the study protocol (e.g. with regard to inclusion and exclusion criteria, physical examination, lab results, etc.) and that the study logistics were properly understood by the investigational team and trial staff.

see 2
Study Types and Study Design

Safety of Enrolled Patients

In accordance with the Declaration of Helsinki, the well-being of the individual patients must certainly take precedence in clinical research over all other interests.

In case of an inadvertent enrolment of an ineligible patient (because of patient fitting exclusion criteria that were overlooked) the sponsor-investigator has to make the decision to discontinue the present therapy, depending on possible risks or harm, in order to guarantee the patient's safety.

Surveillance of Lab Results and Parameters

When the protocol-related procedures include lab testing, those lab results must be reviewed by a study physician for safety reasons: in particular, with regard to flagged, out-of-range values.

For any value outside the normal ranges, the physician must decide if the deviation is clinically relevant or not. If it is clinically relevant, then an AE-CRF should be completed.

It is recommended to assess possible harmful changes in vital signs or other trial-related parameters periodically to assess premature discontinuations.

Advice – Hints and Tips

- Ensure that all regulatory and ethical requirements are fulfilled before starting with the recruitment and screening process.
- Patients must be informed about any screening tests where local regulations may apply (e.g. the HIV-infection test); in these cases, sponsor-investigators may be liable to the obligation to notify authorities.
- Please note that the patient's chronic diseases, medical history, medication, etc. must fit exactly to the appropriate inclusion criteria according to the protocol.
- Make sure that your screening routine is up-to-date and thorough enough to evaluate the eligibility of potential patients.
- Regularly review the clinical records for current diagnoses and lab results to identify recent ineligible patients in order to ensure the well-being of enrolled patients.
- An early monitoring visit at the first patient or first few patients might help avoid technical or logistical protocol violations.

Forms and Templates

- The following template illustrates an Enrolment Log that could possibly be used during the screening process.

⟳ Example: Subject Screening and Enrolment Log

During the entire clinical trial, extensive and multifaceted tasks concerning pharmaco-vigilance have to be planned and carried out.

Therefore, you may consider assigning responsibilities to the pharmaceutical company that e.g. provides you with the IMP and mostly has practice in these duties. The coordination of the tasks should be agreed by contract.

To ensure a mutual understanding, please refer to the following terminology commonly used in pharmacovigilance:

Adverse Event (AE): Any untoward medical occurrence during a clinical trial, not necessarily related to the investigational product.

Adverse Reaction (AR): An adverse medical occurrence related to the investigational product.

Serious Adverse Event (SAE): Adverse events that meet any of the following criteria are identified as SAEs:

- Results in death
- Is life-threatening
- Requires inpatient hospitalization or prolongation of existing hospitalization
- Results in persistent or significant disability/incapacity
- Is a congenital anomaly/birth defect

Serious Adverse Reaction (SAR): A SAE that is related to the investigational product.

Suspected Unexpected Serious Adverse Reaction (SUSAR): An AE, which is suspected to be related to the investigational product and it is not specified in the IB/SmPC as expected.

Prior to study initiation, it is necessary to find out about the safety profile of the study medication. Although you cannot predict every SAE, some ARs to the investigational product might have already been discovered during earlier studies.

It is mandatory that relevant documents, such as the IB or the SmPC, contain information about the product's safety.

Regulatory Reference

- !   ICH GCP Guideline, 6.2.3, 6.8.3, 7.3.6
- !   Detailed Guidance I on EU Directive 2001/20/EC
- !   Detailed guidance on the collection, verification and presentation of adverse reaction reports arising from clinical trials on medicinal products for human use

Responsibilities

Expected Adverse Reactions and Serious Adverse Reactions

Expected ARs and Serious Adverse Reactions (SARs) of the investigational product(s) or medical device(s) must be described in the protocol and the IB/SmPC to get an overview of possible risks and side effects.

The main source for determining ARs/SARs prior to the study is the manufacturer's IB/SmPC. Usually, the information you get from the manufacturer is sufficient.

In case you want to know more about the investigational product, you can use the following sources:

(1) Pharmacovigilance database of the EMA: eudraVigilance. In this database, ARs and SARs are collected internationally. After registration, you can have access authorization to the database via the following link: http://eudravigilance.emea.europa.eu

(2) Findings from preclinical and clinical research: e.g. on medicine databases such as SciSearch or Derwent Drug File. Another possibility to get information about an investigational product is to search in literature meta-databases like Pubmed, Cochrane Library, Biosis Preview or Embase.

In the Investigator's Brochure

The IB contains a summary of ARs that may occur after administration of the investigational product.

see 11
Investigator's Brochure/Summary of Product Characteristics

In the Informed Consent

The sponsor-investigator has the duty to brief the patient accurately on the ARs and SARs that may occur during the planned clinical trial.

The ARs and SARs have to be described completely in the Informed Consent.

see 10
Informed Consent

In the Protocol

In the study protocol, it must be specified in detail, the:

* Definition of all types of AEs/SAEs
* Procedure of reporting AEs/SAEs
* Assessment criteria concerning intensity and causal relationship to the investigational product
* The course of action to record and document AEs/SAEs

see 4
Study Protocol

In the CRF

Certain forms are attached to the CRF that contain specific fields to be completed regarding the occurrence of AEs/SAEs.

see 5
Case Report Forms

Advice – Hints and Tips

Please note especially the differences between the terms Adverse Event and Adverse Reaction, Serious Adverse Event and Serious Adverse Reaction.

Operational Instructions

Refer to the IB/SmPC and learn about all AR/SARs that may occur with your study IMP.

During a clinical trial, it is hard to avoid the occurrence of AEs. The documentation and handling of AEs is defined in the regulatory references below.

Regulatory Reference

- ! ICH GCP Guideline, 4.11, 5.17
- ! EU Directive 2001/20/EC, Art. 16–18
- ! Detailed guidance on the collection, verification and presentation of adverse reaction reports arising from clinical trials on medicinal products for human use
- ! ICH Guideline: Clinical Safety Data Management: Definitions and Standards for Expedited Reporting

Responsibilities

Documentation of Adverse Events
If an AE occurs, it has to be documented immediately:

- In the patient record
- In the CRF on the AE/SAE form

The sponsor-investigator determines, according to regulatory requirements, whether the AE is a SAE. If it is a SAE, it has to be documented additionally on the SAE form in the CRF.

see 5
Case Report Forms

Is the SAE a SUSAR?
The sponsor-investigator has to decide: is the SAE a suspected unexpected and serious adverse reaction (SUSAR)?

The answer is in the affirmative, when the reaction is suspected to be related to the investigational product and it is not specified in the IB/SmPC as expected.

If a SUSAR is determined, specific measures are necessary, which are listed below.

Handling of SUSARs

- Expedited reporting to the regulatory authorities and the Ethics Committee by report form as soon as possible, but definitely within **15 days** (in case of fatal or life-threatening SUSARs, within **7 days**)
- If agreed by contract: expedited reporting to the pharmaceutical company
- *Expedited reporting* to all other investigators as soon as possible
- In case of fatal or life-threatening SUSARs, you have to send a notification about your course of action to the Ethics Committee and the competent authorities in the concerned Member States within an additional **8 days**.

In this chapter's section 'Forms and Templates', you can find a form that contains the content for expedited reporting, which can be used to report SUSARs.

Annual Safety Report

As sponsor-investigator, you have to submit Annual Safety Reports to the Ethics Committee and the competent authorities in the concerned Member States. These safety reports always concern the period of 1 year, if the competent authorities do not demand them earlier.

The first anniversary is exactly 1 year after the approval date of the study authorization. From the anniversary of the study, you have to submit the report within **60 days**. The report contains new safety information and consists of 3 parts:

1. All relevant new findings about effects to the safety of the study population which are not mentioned in the IB/SmPC and an estimation of benefits and risks with a discussion about whether it is necessary to update relevant documents such as the Informed Consent. If you collaborate with a Data Monitoring Committee, you can consult it concerning the risk-benefit assessment.

see 1
Risk-Benefit Analysis

2. Line-listings of all SARs (including SUSARs) that occurred in every involved country:

   - Every event has to be listed once, ordered by system organ classification (SOC) of *MedDRA*. An example listing of the SOC is in this chapter's section 'Forms and Templates'.
   - If several events belong to one person, list all of them and make cross-references.
   - The following 12 necessary points of information must be given in the line-listing:

     (a) Clinical trial identification
     (b) Study participants identification number in the trial
     (c) Case reference number (Case-ID-Number) in the safety database
     (d) Country in which the case occurred
     (e) Age and sex of the trial subject
     (f) Daily dose, dosage form and route of administration of the IMP
     (g) Date of onset of the AR; if not available, a best estimate. For an AR known to occur after cessation of therapy, an estimate of the time lag, if possible
     (h) Dates of treatment
     (i) AR description and interpretation; signs and symptoms can be encoded with MedDRA terminology.

(j) Patient outcome (e.g. resolved, fatal, improved, sequelae, unknown)

(k) Comments, if relevant

(l) Unblinding results, in the case of unblinded SUSARs, that are not declared as expected in the IB/SmPC at the time of their occurrence

3. An aggregate summary tabulation of all SARs (including SUSARs) that occurred, ordered by body system, event and patient group.

In this chapter's section 'Forms and Templates', an example of a line-listing and a summary tabulation is provided.

Advice – Hints and Tips

In all documentation and notifications, the participants have to have a pseudonym with a unique identification number. For more information about the necessity of patient anonymity, see the chapter 'Study Types and Study Design'.

see 2
Study Types and
Study Design

Forms and Templates

◡ Report Form for SUSARs (The form is an interactive PDF-file; you may complete the form with an ordinary PDF-reader).
(http://www.cioms.ch/form/frame_form.htm; accessed January 11, 2011)
◡ Example of a Line Listing
◡ Example of an Aggregate Summary Tabulation
◡ System Organ Classes of MedDRA

After Study

Often the knowledge of the IMP's safety is not complete when the study is closed.

If AEs occur after the study completion for which a relationship with the IMP cannot be excluded, as sponsor-investigator, you are obliged to report those events as part of your clinical trial.

Regulatory Reference

! EU Directive 2001/20/EC, Art. 16–18
! EU Directive 2001/83/EC, Art. 106, 107
! Detailed guidance on the collection, verification and presentation of adverse reaction reports arising from clinical trials on medicinal products for human use

Responsibilities

Final Study Report
In the Final Study Report of a trial, the occurrence of AEs must be described in detail.

see 26
**Final Study Report and
Publication**

Before Initiation

Patient compliance is the ability and the will of the patient to meet the requirements of the study. The compliance can be differentiated into two category groups: (1) the dependability of the patient with respect to the study cooperation (e.g. adherence to doctor's appointments, keeping a diary) and (2) the dependability of the patient's application of the study's investigational drug.

In addition, there exist differences between outpatients without serious illnesses (e.g. hypertension, lipopathy) and inpatients who are more often dangerously ill. Outpatients, particularly employed persons, without serious ailments are less motivated to spend additional time with the study participation duties, e.g. doctor's rounds or checkups such as blood count decreases. The result is that they may become unreliable during the study course or stay completely away from the study. Other inconveniences could be keeping *Quality of Life questionnaires* (because of nature of the private and detailed questions, which, in turn, could cause the feeling of an invasion of privacy), or even complicated medication patterns.

In contrast, inpatients in general have plenty of time, are available and accepting of the frequent and complicated treatments.

Patient compliance is typically good when there are high levels of suffering, poor therapy alternatives, and a promising experimental therapy. If the participant feels negative or no effect (e.g. in placebo group) or is impatient with the drug activity, the compliance could be poor.

Responsibilities

Requirements of the Patient

If an ambulatory patient receives the investigational drug, the packaging should be orientated to the needs of the patient. To improve the compliance, the drug should be taken or administered simply; the packaging should be appealing (such as licensed medicine) and give the impression that it is a professional therapy (common exception: phase I studies or inpatients). The participant has to know, in particular, at what time he/she has to take which drug.

Furthermore, based on the packaging, it should be possible for the sponsor-investigator to hand the patient over only adequate portions of the (labelled) drug (e.g. enough study drug dosage until the next visit). The advantage here is that the sponsor-investigator has the therapy or IMP under control and the subject is reminded of the next check-up.

As sponsor-investigator, you may want to enclose an informational brochure similar to a patient instruction leaflet in every investigational product. This way adverse reactions, dosage information, etc., which are mentioned in the Informed Consent, are clarified once again to the patient. This informational brochure must be submitted to the Ethics Committee.

see 10
Informed Consent

see 19
Pharmacoviligance

Motivation and Fees

Participants or volunteers who take part in a phase I clinical trial usually receive a participant fee, of which the amount has to be approved by the Ethics Committee.

see 14
Ethics

In contrast, patient-participants of a phase II, III or IV clinical trial are not allowed to be paid a fee or be compensated. The reason for this regulation is that these patients have an ailment and they should not be motivated by money for their participation, because this is considered unethical.

In clinical trials with minors, payment is strictly prohibited.

Advice – Hints and Tips

Never underestimate the value of an attractive packaging of the investigational product: a poor compliance could influence the entire study results (especially when considering the generally known unreliability of outpatients).

To support a good compliance, an extensive and detailed conversation with patients could be helpful. This conversation could include:

- Therapy purpose and personal benefit
- Investigational product and benefit
- Consequences of non-administration or non-adherence
- Completing the dialogue with (open) questions related to the understanding of the therapy

Also helpful:

- The use of larger fonts on the packaging/informational brochure to convey important information

During a clinical trial, a poor compliance or ***non-compliance*** in the trial participants is a common issue that directly influences the entire study results.

Below are some reasons for non-compliance and their possible solutions as well as some relevant measurement methods are described.

Regulatory Reference

Not applicable.

Responsibilities

Management of Non-Compliance
In general, any non-compliance of a patient must be adequately followed up by the sponsor-investigator, including proper communication with the patient. This communication must be documented in the patient medical chart.

Some common reasons for non-compliance are explained below.

Patient-Related
- Denial/embarrassment: because patient does not want to be identified or seen as needing medication or participating in a clinical trial, they might transfer the study drug to other containers. This may lead to a loss of information about when and how the medication is supposed to be used, negatively affecting compliance.
- Forgetfulness
- No faith in drug's effectiveness; apathy

Possible Solutions
Frequent follow up is essential for the patient who insists in moving study drug to a neutral container.

In ***calendar-type blister packs and cards***, it is more obvious to the patient whether or not they have taken their medication at the correct time. In addition this makes it harder to 'hide' the study drug; with smart packaging, it can also prevent the loss of dosing and trial information (see below heading 'Blisters versus Bottles').

Is there any kind of follow-up to remind the patient to take their medication as directed? Smart packaging, use of a technique-based diary solution or even an SMS reminder service could help.

Patient education programmes are becoming commonplace in encouraging patients to participate in clinical trials and can help to improve faith and alleviate apathy.

Physical Difficulties
- Swallowing tablets or capsules
- Opening packages

Large packages are inconvenient. Patients may try to remove drug and transfer to a more convenient packaging, negatively affecting compliance.

It is important to choose the smallest capsule size that is possible. The larger a capsule is, the more difficult it is to swallow and the more likely it is for compliance to become an issue.

Small packs/medication units can be difficult for elderly patients to handle. Child-resistant packages are generally more difficult for patients to open.

Some blister designs can make it more difficult to remove medication, because each cavity of one blister is a single protection unit, which is not re-sealable (e.g. the alu/alu formpack: consisting of a formable foil and hard aluminium).

Patients may be more suspicious of adverse events if they do not know what they are taking. Patient/physician education can help (see section 'Patient Compliance – Before Initiation, Advice – Hints and Tips').

see 20
Patient Compliance

Measurement Methods

When evaluating study results, it is always important to know whether the study participants have kept the given therapy pattern as per the protocol, i.e. the dosage per day, or in which extent they have deviated from it.

Therefore, different methods exist such as 'pill counting'/weighing of the remaining quantity (e.g. ointments), clinical support technology, or even the definitive measurement of active substances in the blood/urine. This data should be documented by the sponsor-investigator in the CRF and checked randomly.

see 5
Case Report Forms

'Pill counting' or the assay of active substances in the blood/urine is a valid assessment of the compliance, excluding participants of phase I studies who take their medicine under medical supervision (see section 'Patient Compliance – After Study').

Blisters versus Bottles

There is a significant economic (financial and timeline) advantage of packaging in bottles versus blister packing.

Unfortunately, this gain can be offset by the negative impact on compliance. While bottles may be less expensive, blisters provide the patient with a visual aid to taking their medication correctly. In addition, graphics and dosing instructions can be incorporated into the blister to further aid compliance.

From the sponsor-investigator's perspective, it is far quicker and easier to assess compliance through the presence of unused medication packed in a blister card than to start counting leftover tablets in a bottle. Blister packaging makes the process of identifying and reacting to poor patient compliance much faster and easier.

Electronic Dosage

In some clinical trials, such as phase II studies, the investigational product can be dosed within a box with an electronic cover plate, which records the removal time and amount.

Blood/Urine Analysis

One method of testing the compliance is the measurement of active substances in the blood/urine. Usually, this measurement outcome is only available for a time period directly before the normal concentration decrease and not for the entire clinical trial.

Advice – Hints and Tips

Bear in mind the following that may affect patient compliance:

- The possible necessity of child-resistant or senior-friendly packaging
- The reality of multi-lingual labelling for multinational clinical trials

- Complex medication patterns can result in a high number of units taken each day by the patient (particularly in clinical trials when comparator products and double-dummy designs are used)

In this chapter, the early steps of the clinical trial evaluation with regard to compliance and drug exposure are described.

Regulatory Reference

Not applicable.

Responsibilities

Pill Counting/IMP Weighing

'Pill counting' or weighing of the remaining IMP that the patient has given back, is a possibility for the sponsor-investigator to document the ingested amount of the investigational drug and the deviation from the dispensed amount.

see 3
Investigational Medicinal Product

Regarding the **biometrical evaluation**, it should be determined what relevant deviation of the actual value from the desired value is defined in the study protocol (e.g. give or take 20% of the desired value). Additionally, it should be specified how participants with relevant deviations and those who do not give their drug back be evaluated.

see 24
Biometry

see 4
Study Protocol

The negative aspects of this method include:

- An analytically correct amount of the ingested amount of the investigational drug does not warrant an absolute certainty
- In cases of a deviation of the ingested amount, it remains unknown which dosage per day the subject has been taking

Classification of the Compliance

Referring to the biometrical evaluation, it could be helpful to divide the participants into sub-classes, e.g. reluctance, average and good compliance. This classification is universally applicable for all measurement methods.

Source Data Verification (SDV) is a required process to set up the reliability and evaluation of the collected data in clinical studies.

Regulatory Reference

! ICH GCP Guideline, Chapter 5.18.4

Responsibilities

Purpose
SDV is a process to verify CRF-entries against data in the source documents (original documents, data and records). Performed by the Monitor at each site-monitoring visit, all deviations and discrepancies in the data have to be documented and reported to the sponsor-investigator and related staff.

Source Data Verification and Related Activities
The following issues describe the sponsor-investigator's responsibilities related to SDV. This procedure is completed upon the initial review of the CRF and attached to the Site Monitoring Report:

see 23
Monitoring

Initial verification of critical data (completed during first Site Monitoring Visit):

* Informed consent obtained prior to inclusion in study
* Visit date(s) as available
* Eligibility criteria
* Medical history
* Medication history

Ongoing verification of critical data (completed during subsequent site monitoring visits):

* Visit date
* AEs
* SAEs
* Concomitant medications
* Study drug dispensing
* Answered queries pertaining to key efficacy parameters, changes re-confirmed with the source documents
* Primary efficacy data

Ongoing verification of non-critical data, if needed (to be completed during subsequent site monitoring visits).

Forms and Templates

◑ Source Data Verification Form

22 Quality

A high standard of quality is fundamental for a successful outcome to any clinical trial. The implementation of quality systems should be planned carefully and in detail.

Regulatory Reference

! ICH GCP Guideline, Chapters 1.46, 1.47, 1.55, 1.6, 1.8, 1.38, 1.39, 1.55, 5.1
! EU Directive 2001/20/EC, Art. 1.2
! EU Directive 2005/28/EC, Chapter 1, Art. 2.4

Responsibilities

Standard Operating Procedures

The amount of data would increase considerably if any procedure is analyzed in too much detail, or if too much information is collected for describing the study's results; furthermore, it would be too obtrusive.

Fortunately, many trial procedures are similar or even the same and, thus, it is recommended to use Standard Operating Procedures (SOPs). They can be simply a written document/list of instructions, detailing all the steps and activities of a process to come up with a standard way of implementing a specific function. Thus, SOPs can be used for every trial (exceptions are allowed) and a large part of the quality assurance programme.

There are no specific requirements for SOP organization or categories made by the regulations. Nevertheless, the following categorization is useful.

- Administration (e.g. the creation of a Master SOP, SOPs for training and the administration and archiving of SOPs)
- Planning (e.g. obtaining the IB, procedures to find out specific regulatory requirements of the country where the study will take place, the evaluation of the study sites, and the content and structure of the visit reports)
- Documentation and procedures regarding the allocation and enrolment of the participants and their randomization
- Structure and content of a study protocol, amendments, CRFs and the declaration of consent (plus its translation to the participants native language) and Procedures that can be used to notice if CRFs are missing as well as procedures to find those lost CRFs
- Monitoring (e.g. a pre-study visit and other monitoring visits as well as the content and structure of the monitoring reports)
- Documentation (e.g. content and structure of the TMF)
- Handling of study material (e.g. procedures regarding the IMP, labelling or the handling of blood samples)
- Drug safety (e.g. documentation of AEs or the annual safety report)
- Authorities (e.g. the communication with the responsible authority or the preparation and escort of inspections)
- Interaction and communication (e.g. with an independent Data Monitoring Committee or with external contract partners such as laboratories)
- Data management and biometry (e.g. the input and correction of trial-related data, access authority to the study database and its structure and validation)

All these SOPs give a comprehensive picture of the structure of the study's workflows as well as the responsibilities for the documentation of a trial.

It is necessary to train each employee that will work with a SOP before they will make use of it. The training may be conducted in many ways. Regardless whether the employee gained his knowledge from a presentation, a video conference or a single training, a verification that the employee passed the training module should be documented and be on hand. The aim of these trainings is not to merely repeat its content but rather to understand the corresponding procedure by asking questions, discussing ambiguities and exchange experiences.

Quality Control

The control of the trial's quality includes any operational measurements and actions used within the quality assurance system. The aim is to confirm that the quality requirements of any activity concerning the trial have been considered.

The quality should be checked at each step of data handling to guarantee the reliability of the data and that all records have been processed correctly.

Monitoring and Auditing

see 23
Monitoring

Independent monitoring is often the key to guarantee the study's quality and, therefore, it is an essential role. Nevertheless, always keep in mind: intense monitoring causes great cost.

In addition to monitoring, auditing is an important aspect for the quality assurance of the trial. Auditing is a systematic and independent inspection of any trial-related activities and documents. Its purpose is to find out whether the inspected activities were conducted accurately and whether the data were recorded, analyzed and correctly reported in accordance with the SOPs (as well as the study protocol and GCP).

see 4
Study Protocol

Advice – Hints and Tips

- Check if the already written SOPs could fit to your study. Use them!
- Check how detailed the monitoring needs to be beforehand to save money.

In all phases of the study, the quality has to be in accordance with the standards given in the GCP. A well-documented trial is the basis for ensuring the study's quality.

As you already know: anything that was not documented did not happen. Therefore, it is essential that any technique used to ensure the quality of a trial, such as the training of employees regarding the use of SOPs, is documented and available at any time.

Regulatory Reference

! ICH GCP Guideline, Chapters 1.46, 1.47, 1.55, 5.1
! EU Directive 2001/20/EC, Art. 1.2
! EU Directive 2005/28/EC, Chapter 1, Art. 2.4

Responsibilities

Standard Operating Procedures

The sponsor-investigator is responsible for creating and keeping the quality assurance and the quality control systems with the written SOPs. He has to make sure that the study is in compliance with the protocol, the GCP, plus the regulatory requirements and that the data is generated, documented and reported correctly.

If an SOP is missing, generate an SOP that is fitting to your study.

Quality Control

After every phase of the study, the sponsor-investigator has to complete the reporting requirements for the quality control to guarantee the completeness and correctness of the data.

Monitoring and auditing reports give information whether the trial is compliant to the sponsor's SOPs (if applicable) and are provided to the sponsor after every contact regarding the trial (e.g. a site visit or other study-related communication).

Advice – Hints and Tips

- The SOPs should be carried out without any deviation or change.
- If the SOP is not followed correctly, the expected result cannot be guaranteed. Any change or variation from a given SOP should be carefully investigated and results of that investigation should be documented.
- It is recommended to update SOPs frequently to guarantee conformity to the regulatory requirements and the working practice (usually every second year).
- Bear in mind: a training upgrade of the employees is necessary if the modification of the SOP was substantial.

It is very important to document in detail every procedure and step made during a clinical trial.

With regard to the SOPs, it is essential to document any change or deviation made on a given SOP; furthermore, it must be documented prior to initiation. In general, modifications are caused by procedural change and/or adjustments.

After Study

Regulatory Reference

!   ICH GCP Guideline, Chapter 1.55

Responsibilities

Standard Operating Procedures

In some cases, it can happen that a SOP does not exist yet or has to be modified to fit the trial. In order to have a full list of SOPs used in the concerned trial, the sponsor-investigator may create a SOP Manual as an overview to summarize all Quality Systems Documents used in the trial.

At this point, a Manual has to be prepared and includes the following 3 steps:
1. Review the study through intense communication with anyone who was involved in the trial's process to understand in detail the actual procedure that was performed
2. Preparation of a draft manual
3. Finalization of the draft manual after talking to the users (see step 1); lastly, inaccuracies are corrected, suggestions and references are discussed and accepted or rejected.

The manual should contain information about the *main topics*, the *organization structure* that shows the hierarchical relationships in the organization for which the manual is prepared and the process such as the data management.

Usually SOPs are administered electronically to save space for storage and to update them easier and faster. A paper-based administration is possible, too; it is generally used by administrators of smaller trials who are concerned to save money by omitting the electronic data management of SOPs.

It is possible to write global SOPs (ones that theoretically could be used on every location in the world), but to adapt them to the local requirements (the authorities' requirements vary in each nation, particularly with regard to certain items, such as pharmacovigilance).

Advice – Hints and Tips

* If all processes and procedures concerning the quality are laid out in SOPs, they can be used as the basis for a routine training programme of employees.
* Bear in mind: too many SOPs could lead to a collapse of the SOP System! Therefore, the structure of a SOP System and the full amount of individual SOPs should be considered carefully.

Forms and Templates

◔ Example: SOP Template

Trial monitoring is an important component to ensure patient safety and completeness and correctness of the gained data in clinical studies. Subject to the regulations of ICH GCP, a Site Initiation Visit (SIV) has to take place before a clinical trial begins. This SIV is performed to review the final protocol, the IB and regulatory requirements with the sponsor-investigator and related staff, and to instruct study personnel in study procedures, including patient recruitment, informed consent, drug dispensing and accountability, and CRF completion.

[handwritten margin notes: • patient safety • completeness + correctness of gained data]

Regulatory Reference

!   ICH GCP Guideline, Chapter 5.6

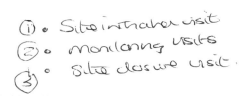

[handwritten margin notes: ① • Site initiation visit ② • monitoring visits ③ • Site closure visit.]

Responsibilities

Purpose   ①
The SIV has to be performed by the Monitor. He/she has to take care that all relevant study staff is present at the site initiation meeting to ensure that all study personnel will be sufficiently informed of all responsibilities. Unsolved issues have to be discussed with the sponsor-investigator. The SIV begins prior any study activities, which means even before subject enrolment.

Prior to the Site Initiation Visit
The following steps have to be completed before the SIV:

- Determining the outstanding regulatory documents
- Planning the visit with the sponsor-investigator and study personnel
- Writing a confirmation letter for the purpose of the visit, issues to be discussed and the collection of any outstanding regulatory documents
- Arranging study material such as procedure manuals, a sample CRF, etc.
- Arranging drug shipment to site

Conducting the Site Initiation Visit
The following outline describes the responsibilities during the visit and is directly from the ICH GCP guidance document.

1. RESPONSIBILITIES OF THE SPONSOR-INVESTIGATOR
   (Have been discussed with the Sponsor-Investigator and relevant staff?)

   1.1 Trial Conduct according as per ICH GCP guidelines?
   1.2 Compliance with the protocol?
   1.3 Recruitment rate?
   1.4 Instructions on study specific procedures?
   1.5 Randomization procedures or allocation and unblinding?
   1.6 Patient information and Informed Consent procedures of Trial Participants?
   1.7 Documentation and reliability of the data (complete, accurate, accessible)?

1.8 Progress reports to Ethics Committee?
1.9 Procedures for subject/study discontinuation?
1.10 Current Sponsor-Investigator Drug Brochure?

2. INVESTIGATIONAL MEDICINAL PRODUCT (STUDY DRUG)

2.1 Was the study drug and storage area discussed?
2.2 Were ordering and control procedures discussed?
2.3 Were dispensing, dose modification, accountability discussed?
2.4 Were storage conditions discussed?
2.5 Was return and destruction discussed?
2.6 Is the expiry date compatible with the study duration?
2.7 Are there sufficient study drug supplies available and stored appropriately?
2.8 Have code break envelopes been delivered, inspected and stored appropriately?

3. ADVERSE EVENTS (AE) AND SERIOUS ADVERSE EVENTS (SAE)
(Have they been discussed with the Sponsor-Investigator and relevant staff?)

3.1 Description of AE and SAE
3.2 Reporting requirements
3.3 Documenting
3.4 Reporting regular safety updates, safety alerts and AEs and/or SAEs to Ethics Committee in accordance to local requirements

4. CASE REPORT FORMS (CRFs)
(Have they been discussed with the Sponsor-Investigator and relevant staff?)

4.1 Completion of the CRFs
4.2 Correction the CRFs
4.3 Flow of CRFs (completion, collection, and shipping)
4.4 Flow of queries type I/II

5. OTHER STUDY SUPPLIES

5.1 Are other supporting materials available?
5.2 Is the material and quantity adequate?
5.3 Is the material appropriately stored?

6. MONITORING
(Has it been discussed with the Sponsor-Investigator and relevant staff?)

6.1 Monitoring frequency
6.2 Monitoring procedures
6.3 Time required for monitoring visits
6.4 Time availability of site staff
6.5 Have relevant source documents been specified and discussed?
6.6 Working space availability
6.7 Has the type, frequency and documentation of communication between the investigational site and sponsor (or monitor) been established and agreed upon?

7. FACILITIES/LABORATORY

7.1 Have there been change(s) in the facilities/study site staff?
If yes, have staff been appropriately trained and all required documentation updated?
7.2 Was the laboratory visited?
7.3 Are the reference ranges valid?
7.4 Are the laboratory certificates valid?
7.5 Are the central laboratory ranges current?
7.6 Are the central laboratory certificates current?

8. BIOLOGICAL SAMPLES

8.1 Has the storage area been inspected?
8.2 Are site staff familiar with sample taking, labelling and storage procedures?
8.3 Are site staff familiar with the sampling handling and shipment procedure?
8.4 Is the freezer log or other required temperature controls available and adequate?
8.5 Are there sufficient supplies available?

9. TRIAL MASTER FILE

9.1 Was the Trial Master File reviewed?
9.2 Are all required documents filed in the Trial Master File?

10. ARCHIVING

10.1 Has document storage and archiving been discussed and agreed to?

Follow-Up to the Site Initiation Visit
The following tasks have to be completed after the SIV:
- Follow-up letter to the sponsor-investigator of the visit's outcome
- Write up a SIV Report (supply as attachment to letter)
- Copy of the report must be placed in the TMF

Advice – Hints and Tips

- SIVs should be performed only by individuals at the level of Monitor/Clinical Research Associate or above.
- In case there is no Monitor available, the sponsor-investigator should check if all requirements are fulfilled and should document this on the form (see the Site Initiation Visit Report Form, in this chapter's 'Forms and Templates' section).

Forms and Templates

↻ Site Initiation Visit Report Form

For the duration of the trial, periodic Site Monitoring Visits (SMV) need to be conducted. These interim visits are intended to ensure the trial is conducted in compliance with the study protocol, all regulations and ICH GCP guidelines. Additionally, all facilities and related staff must be examined in order to determine an acceptable level of training for the conduct of the study.

Regulatory Reference

!   ICH GCP Guideline, Chapter 5.18

Responsibilities

Purpose
Performed by the Monitor, SMVs must take place periodically based on the following:

- Number of participants in the study
- Study design
- Number of problems encountered
- Disease being treated

Prior to the Monitoring Visit
The following tasks must be completed before each SMV:

- Schedule a visit with the sponsor-investigator and related personnel
- Write a confirmation letter of the purpose of the visit and the issues to be discussed
- Review previous Site Monitoring Reports (if any) regarding outstanding items or issues that need attention
- Review outstanding data management issues
- Review outstanding laboratory issues
- Review reported SAEs
- Review drop-outs

Conducting the Site Monitoring Visit
The following outline describes the responsibilities during the visit and is directly from the ICH GCP guidance document.

1. PROTOCOL ADHERENCE

- Have there been any protocol (including amendments) violation(s)?
- For each subject, has an Informed Consent been properly obtained and documented?
- Is the recruitment rate satisfactory?

2. CLINICIAL SAFETY

- Were there any **NEW** SAEs reported since the previous visit?
- If yes, have all new SAEs been completely and correctly reported?
- Have all **NEW** non-serious AEs, which resulted in permanent discontinuation, been completely and correctly reported?
- Is the randomization/treatment allocation procedure being followed?

3. CASE REPORT FORMS

- Were CRFs reviewed and source document verification performed during this visit?
- Were CRFs consistent with source documents?
- Were all required source documents available?
- Is the CRF quality acceptable?
- Is the study site up to date with CRF completion?
- Were any CRFs collected during this visit?
- Were queries reviewed, answered, signed, dated and collected during this visit?

4. INVESTIGATIONAL PRODUCT

- Was the study drug and storage area inspected at this visit?
- Is the study drug correctly stored and dispensed in accordance with the protocol requirements?
- Is the study drug accountability procedure correctly performed?
- Does the expiry date remain compatible with the study duration?
- Is there sufficient study drug supply available for study continuation?
- Is the blind maintained (code-break envelopes inspected and intact)?

5. FACILITIES/LABORATORY

- Have there been change(s) in the facilities/study site staff?
- Have there been changes in normal laboratory values/ranges or diagnostic instruments?

6. BIOLOGICAL SAMPLES

- Are the biological samples appropriately labelled and stored?
- Is the site staff familiar with sampling handling procedure?
- Is the freezer log or other required temperature controls maintained?
- Are there sufficient supplies available for continuation of the study?

7. TRIAL MASTER FILE

- Was the Trial Master File reviewed?
- Are all required documents filed in the Trial Master File and available for review?

Follow-Up to the Monitoring Visit

The following tasks have to be completed after the SMV:
- Follow-up letter to the Sponsor-Investigator of the visit's outcome
- Write up a Site Monitoring Visit Report (provide as attachment to letter)
- Copy of the report must be placed in the TMF

Advice – Hints and Tips

- SMVs should be performed only by individuals at the level of Monitor/Clinical Research Associate or above.
- In case there is no Monitor available, the sponsor-investigator should check that all requirements are fulfilled and should document this on the form (see the Site Monitoring Visit Report Form, in this chapter's section 'Forms and Templates').
- SMVs have to be performed at least once yearly.

Forms and Templates

↻ Site Monitoring Visit Report Form

After Study

At the conclusion of the trial, Site Closure Visits (SCV) must be carried out to ensure the completion and accuracy of the study records and data, to retrieve completed study records and regulatory documents and, lastly, to verify the proper disposition of the study drug.

All site staff should be informed and know for how long trial documents must be kept and archived (records retention requirements).

Regulatory Reference

! ICH GCP Guideline, Chapter 5.18

Responsibilities

Purpose
SCVs, performed by the Monitor, must take place after the last subject finishes the study or at the final Site Monitoring Visit. Some of the following issues may be accomplished at the end of the trial during the Site Monitoring Visit.

Prior to the Close-Out Visit
The following tasks must be completed before the SCV:
- Schedule a visit with the sponsor-investigator and related personnel
- Write a confirmation letter of the purpose of the visit and the issues to be discussed
- Review requirements for the return or destruction of the study drug
- Review any previous Site Closure Reports on outstanding items or issues that need attention
- Review outstanding data management issues
- Review outstanding laboratory issues

- Review reported SAEs
- Review drop-outs
- Arrange the completion and availability for retrieval of all remaining documents, including CRFs, Data Clarification Forms, laboratory reports, drug dispensing and return records, and final SAE information

Conducting the Site Closure Visit

The following outline describes the responsibilities during the visit and is directly from the ICH GCP guidance document.

1. PROTOCOL ADHERENCE

    1.1   Have there been any changes in the documented protocol violation since the last visit?

2. CLINICAL SAFETY

    2.1   Has the Ethics Committee received "the trial outcome summary", reviewing the safety and efficacy of the trial?

3. CASE REPORT FORMS

    3.1   Have there been any changes since the previous visit?

4. INVESTIGATIONAL PRODUCT

    4.1   Have there been any changes since the previous visit?

5. FACILITIES/LABORATORY

    5.1   Have there been any changes since the previous visit?

6. BIOLOGICAL SAMPLES

6.1 Have all stored biological samples been shipped to either a central or local laboratory since the previous visit?

7. REGULATORY AFFAIRS

    7.1   Has the sponsor-investigator received "the trial outcome summary", reviewing the safety and efficacy of the trial?

8. TRIAL MASTER FILE

    8.1 Does the Trial Master File remain up to date, securely stored?

Follow-Up to the Site Closure Visit

The following tasks must be completed after the SCV:

- Follow-up letter to the sponsor-investigator of the visit's outcome
- Draw up a SCV Report (see the Site Closure Visit Report Form, in this chapter's 'Forms and Templates' section, below)
- Copy of the report must be placed in the TMF

Advice – Hints and Tips

- SCVs should be performed only by individuals at the level of Monitor/Clinical Research Associate or above.
- If there is no Monitor available, the sponsor-investigator should check whether all requirements are met and should document this on the Site Closure Visit Report Form (see the Site Closure Visit Report Form, in this chapter's section 'Forms and Templates').

Forms and Templates

○ Site Closure Visit Report Form

This chapter focuses mainly on statistical principles, since specific statistical procedures and methods that ensure the implementation of these principles fall under the responsibility of the sponsor-investigator.

Generally, the goal of most of these principles lies in minimizing bias and maximizing precision. In ICH GCP and the EU Directives, it is assumed that the statistical parts of the trial are dealt with by an appropriately qualified and experienced statistician, namely, the trial statistician.

Regulatory Reference

!   ICH Harmonized Tripartite Guideline Topic E9 Statistical Principles for Clinical Trials

Responsibilities

All relevant statistical issues should be covered in the study protocol and any amendments. Ideally, this would be the trial statistician's job.

Primary Variables
This is the variable that provides the most relevant and convincing evidence regarding the primary objective of the clinical trial. In most cases, it will probably be an efficacy variable, but safety/tolerability, quality of life or health economics are also potential primary variables. Its selection, clinical relevance, and measurement procedures need to be described and justified in the study protocol with sufficient evidence.

In some cases, the primary variable may be a composite variable (a combination of multiple clinical measurements) or a global assessment variable (a combination of objective variables and the sponsor-investigator's overall impression of the state or change in state of a patient). It is also possible to use multiple primary variables, surrogate variables (if direct measurement of clinical effects is not practical) or categorized variables (e.g. reduction of diastolic blood pressure below 90 mmHg). All these variable types need to be further addressed and justified in the study protocol.

Avoiding Bias
Randomisation and blinding are the most common design techniques to avoid or minimize bias.

see 2
Study Types and
Study Design

Trial Design Considerations
The most common designs for confirmatory trials are parallel-group designs. Less common are crossover or factorial designs (two or more treatments evaluated simultaneously).

Type of Comparison
Most investigator-initiated trials will try to demonstrate superiority to placebo using a placebo-controlled trial, superiority to an active-control treatment or by demonstrating a dose-response relationship. These trials are referred to as trials to show superiority. Other types of comparison are trials to show equivalence or non-inferiority, as well as trials that establish a dose-response relationship.

Sample Size

The appropriate number of participants in the clinical trial depends on the following factors: the primary variable, the test statistic, the null hypothesis, the alternative/working hypothesis, the probability of erroneously rejecting the null hypothesis (type I error), the probability of erroneously failing to reject the null hypothesis (type II error), and the approach to dealing with treatment withdrawals and protocol violations.

The calculating method for the sample size should be stated in the study protocol, as well as the quantity estimates used in the method (variances, mean values, etc.). In most cases, the probability of the type I error should be set at 5%, and the probability of the type II error at 10% to 20%. Depending on the type II error, i.e. the power is 90% to 80%, respectively. It is in the interest of the sponsor-investigator to keep the probability of the type II error as low as possible.

Analysis

The principal features of the analysis should be already described in the statistical section of the study protocol. The (detailed) analysis plan itself may be a separate document, which may be written after the study protocol but **before** breaking the blind. The final statistical plan and its date should be formally recorded.

Ideally, all randomized participants in a clinical trial would have satisfied all the entry criteria, followed all trial procedures without any losses to follow-up and had complete data records. Since this is always attempted but almost never attained in reality, the statistical section of the study protocol should specify procedures to deal with problems considering missing values, protocol violations and withdrawals.

Estimation, Confidence Interval and Hypothesis Testing

The hypotheses that are to be tested and/or the treatment effects to be estimated to provide evidence considering the primary objective should be written down in the statistical section of the study protocol. The statistical methods and models intended to achieve this using the primary variable need to be described as well.

Furthermore, the use of one- and two-sided tests of statistical significance needs to be clarified; in particular, the use of a one-sided test needs to be justified. Generally, the chosen statistical methods should reflect the current state of medicinal and statistical knowledge, considering the to-be-analyzed variable and the statistical model.

Advice – Hints and Tips

The study sample size should be at least 10% greater than the estimated sample size to adequately deal with withdrawals.

This chapter covers problems occurring during a study that involve statistical consequences.

Regulatory Reference

! ICH Harmonized Tripartite Guideline Topic E9 Statistical Principles for Clinical Trials

Responsibilities

Changes in Exclusion and Inclusion Criteria

Normally, these criteria should stay constant during a trial. However, growing medical knowledge, interim analysis, repeated violations of the entry criteria or low-recruitment rates may suggest a change of the criteria. These changes need to be described by a protocol amendment that includes the statistical consequences. The changes should also be accomplished without breaking the blind.

Sample Size Adjustment

In some cases, a blinded data interim check may reveal that the original design and sample size calculations need to be revised. This needs to be explained and justified in a protocol amendment, while preserving the data blind.

Interim Analysis and Early Stopping

Any analysis intending to compare treatment arms before the formal completion of a trial is considered an interim analysis. An interim analysis is either already planned and described in the study protocol or dictated by special circumstances, which require a protocol amendment describing the analysis. This amendment must be completed prior to the unblinded access to the treatment data.

Acceptable reasons for interim analysis and to decide whether to terminate a trial are:

- Superiority of the treatment under study is clearly established
- Demonstration of a relevant treatment difference has become unlikely
- Unacceptable adverse effects have appeared

If an interim analysis is executed, it should be handled confidentially. Only the staff handling the analysis should be informed. The other staff should stay blinded and unaware of the analysis to prevent inadvertent modification of the attitude towards the trial, bias in treatment comparison or changes in the characteristics of the patients to be recruited.

Any unplanned or not appropriately planned interim analysis may result in flawed results and/or weaken the confidence in drawn conclusions. Therefore, this possible impact needs to be included in the study report.

Advice – Hints and Tips

For any unplanned interim analysis, remember to recalculate the sample size.

This chapter covers the statistical analysis of the data and the reporting of the statistical work.

Regulatory Reference

!   ICH Harmonized Tripartite Guideline Topic E9 Statistical Principles for Clinical Trials

Responsibilities

Data Analysis Considerations

In general, there are two sets in which the data of a trial can be analyzed.

If all randomized participants are included, it is an intention-to-treat set. The other possible set, the per-protocol set, is a subgroup of the intention-to-treat set which comprises the participants who are fully compliant with the study protocol. In most cases, the sponsor-investigator should try to conduct the statistical analysis on both sets.

Reporting

After conducting the trial, a blinded review of the planned analysis as written in the study protocol may be valuable. This blinded review should be made by staff not involved in any prior unblinded (e.g. interim) analysis in order to avoid bias.

see 26
Final Study Report and
Publication

Adhering to the planned analysis as outlined in the study protocol enhances the credibility of the results. Any deviations should be carefully explained and justified. In addition, protocol violations, withdrawals from treatment and losses of participants or data need to be considered.

Tables and/or graphical representations of the descriptive statistics should be an indispensible part of the report.

Multicentre trials constitute a great hurdle for the scientists and physicians involved. The clinical, methodical, and ethical requirements are much greater than in a single-centre trial.

On the other hand, the validity of multicentre trials is often greater because they implicate a larger number of participants, have more geographic locations with the possibility of inclusion of a wider range of population groups, and the ability to compare results among centres. Often the efficacy of a medical product varies significantly between the study groups because of different genetic, environmental, and ethnic or cultural backgrounds. Most of the large clinical trials, usually phase-III trials, are multicentre trials.

Multicentre trials are similar to single-centre trials; nevertheless, the tasks of multicentre trials are more extensive. A multicentre trial can take place nationally or internationally. The study procedure is typically set in a general protocol that is valid for every participating study centre.

Please consider carefully if you, in your role as sponsor-investigator, are able to supervise an international clinical trial.

Regulatory Reference

!   ICH GCP Guideline, Chapters 5.23, 5.6.1
!   EU Directive 2001/20/EC, Art. 2b, Art. 7

Responsibilities

Kinds of Investigators
Coordinating Investigator
In multicentre trials, there is one coordinating investigator who is responsible to coordinate all the investigators at all the participating trial centres. The coordinating investigator could be an investigator himself or someone who is invested in being a coordinating investigator.

Functions and duties of the coordinating investigator may include:

* Summoning a study commission
* Development and proposal of the therapy concept
* Discussion, voting within the study commission
* Preparation of the study protocol
* Submission of the study protocol to the IEC in every participating country
* Establishment and organization of the study central
* Nomination of a representative
* Survey and accomplishment of the study protocol
* Distribution of the study protocol to all sites involved
* Survey of the study course, termination criteria
* Application of financial sponsorship of the trial
* Coordination of the involved reference-institutions

- Nomination and management of a DMC
- Coordination of the research project
- Allocation of data/materials for the research project
- Exchange of experience with international study groups

Investigator

There is always one investigator (perhaps supported by sub-investigators) in every different centre. They are responsible to let the coordinating investigator know all trial-related events that happened at their trial centre. All investigators have to adhere to the approved protocol.

Coordinating Committee

Nomination of a committee is permitted, one which is able to organize and coordinate the several trial centres.

Advice – Hints and Tips

Responsibilities of the coordinating investigator and all other involved investigators must be documented before the initiation of the trial.

All investigators are instructed how to comply with the protocol in order to achieve a unified standard in the documentation of clinical and laboratory findings and the completion of the CRFs.

The number of patients must be documented and justified for every trial centre.

If the multicentre trial is located in different countries, it must be demonstrated that a positive vote is obtained from each of the health authorities and local Ethics Committee in each country where the trial will be conducted.

The successful accomplishment of a multicentre trial requires exhaustive instruction of the medical personnel and a detailed design of the study procedure. For certain, a high-quality monitoring programme is required during the whole implementation, with a central – and preferably independent – capture and evaluation of the gathered data.

Regulatory Reference

! ICH GCP Guideline, Chapters 5.23, 5.61

Responsibilities

Functions and Duties of the Coordinating Investigator
- Survey and accomplishment of the study protocol
- Consultation of study participants on the accomplishment of the study protocol and in problematic cases
- Preparation of interim reports for the study commission and the study participants
- Organization and conduction of workshop-meetings
- Survey of the study course, termination criteria
- Coordination of the involved reference-institutions
- Preparation of interim reports for the DMC
- Timely notice of termination of study involvement prior to study closure

see 19
Pharmacoviligance

Functions and Duties of Investigators at Each Study Centre
- Immediate report of AEs, SAEs and SUSARs to the **coordinating investigator** and the study's Ethics Committee

Advice – Hints and Tips

It has to be clearly written in the study protocol, which information each investigator has to transfer.

The CRFs must be created in such a way as to ensure that all required data could be comprehended and entered completely and accurately at every trial centre.

When a multicentre trial is closed, all the collected data should be analyzed as a whole to be comparable to the results of other studies.

Indeed, every centre has its own results; however, the data are only of importance and should be presented, e.g. when all the centres have a sufficient number of patients to make an analysis potentially valuable.

Extreme values at a study centre should be discussed and adequately noted.

Regulatory Reference

! ICH GCP Guideline, Chapter 5.23

see 26
Final Study Report and Publication

Responsibilities

Functions and Duties of Coordinating Investigator
Publication of study results.

After Study

A clinical trial is not truly complete until the final study report and its publication is released. This publication contains much more than just statistical and clinical data. It can be seen as providing the far-reaching implications of the trial.

The final study report includes clinical and statistical explanations, presentations, and analyses that are integrated in a single report, the so-called 'integrated full report'. It incorporates the tables and charts, the description of the participants, the analysis of the dropouts, and the definition of the efficiency and compatibility of the product, to give the conclusion and the significance of the trial.

Regulatory Reference

! ICH GCP Guideline E3: Note for Guidance on Structure and Content of Clinical Study Reports (CPMP/ICH/137/95), July 1996.
! The Consort Statement: Revised Recommendations for Improving the Quality of Reports of Parallel-Group Randomized Trials
! Declaration of Helsinki

Responsibilities

Formal Requirements of the Final Study Report

For the correct closure of the trial, a summary of the Final Study Report according to the template provided below must be sent to the responsible regulatory authorities as well as to the Ethics Committee(s). This summary or synopsis has to contain all the relevant outcomes of the study.

The Final Study Report is written in close cooperation with all people that took part in the trial, such as the sponsor or biometricians. Therefore, it is very important to pay attention to the deadline, which is usually one year after the end date of the study, to make sure that everyone who is involved can send the required data in time.

The structure of the Final Study Report is strictly specified. The report is divided into the following sections:

1. Title Page
2. Synopsis
3. Table of Contents (for the individual clinical study report)
4. List of Abbreviations and Definition of Terms
5. Ethics
6. Investigators and Study Administrative Structure
7. Introduction
8. Study Objectives
9. Investigational Plan
10. Study Patients
11. Efficacy Evaluation
12. Safety Evaluation
13. Discussion and Overall Conclusions

14. Tables, Figures and Graphs (referred to but not included in the text)
15. Reference List
16. Appendices

The analysis is considered complete after all these topics are written down in an integrated report, regardless whether or not the trial was finished as scheduled. Depending on the importance and duration of a study, a less detailed Final Report might be suitable. For the detailed structure and content, see the form, 'Structure and Content Final Report' in this chapter's section 'Forms and Templates'.

Publication

In general, any clinical trial and its results should be published.

In light of this, the CONSORT Statement (CONsolidated Standards of Reporting Trials) must be considered. The statement is used to give the reader a better understanding of a trial's design, performance, analysis and explanation, and to evaluate the validity of its outcomes. It is also used as a standard method for authors to set up a better reporting of, for example, a randomized controlled trial (RCT).

For other study types, extensions of the CONSORT Statement have been developed with detailed designs, figures and interventions.

For a publication, the following checklist and flow diagram should be used. The current versions can be viewed and downloaded on the website (http://www.consort-statement.org/).

Title and Abstract (1.)

Introduction
  2. Background

Methods
  3. Trial design
  4. Participants
  5. Interventions
  6. Outcomes
  7. Sample size
Randomization:
  8. Sequence generation
  9. Allocation concealment mechanism
10. Implementation
11. Blinding
12. Statistical methods

Results
13. Participant flow (a diagram is strongly recommended)
14. Recruitment
15. Baseline data
16. Numbers analyzed

17. Outcomes and estimation
18. Ancillary analyses
19. Harms

Discussion
20. Limitations
21. Generalisability
22. Interpretation

Other information
23. Registration
24. Protocol
25. Funding

The purpose of a **flow diagram** is to clearly show the number of patients who participated in the RCT and their disposition. The following flow diagram shows 4 stages of a trial (Enrolment, Allocation, Follow-up and Analysis) and gives information about the number of participants in each intervention cluster.

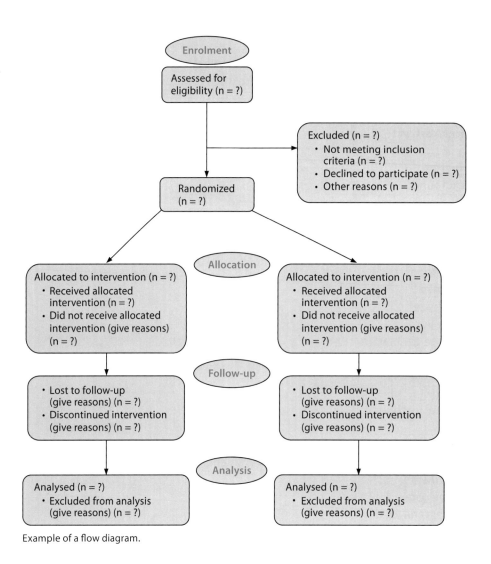

Example of a flow diagram.

Advice – Hints and Tips

- Consider using the current CONSORT Statement when publishing results as a good publication practice
- Keep in mind that the requirements of the responsible regulatory authority or the Ethics Committee(s) can vary the length of the report. The requests vary in each country. Discuss an appropriate report format with your authority.
- Appoint the responsibilities for each section of the Report as well as the persons that sign the Report in advance.
- The name, telephone and fax number of the sponsor's contact persons for questions arising during the review of the Study Report should be indicated on the title page or in the letter of application.
- For the Synopsis, several sections might be copied from the Annual Safety Report.
- If other studies used an extremely comparable protocol, it might be helpful to make a note of this and describe any significant differences in the section 'Overall Study Design and Plan – Descriptions' (section 9.1).
- Important: always pay attention to deadlines!

Forms and Templates

◔ Structure and Content Final Report

Common Abbreviations

AE   = Adverse event
AR   = Adverse reaction
CA   = Competent Authority
CRF   = Case Report Form
CTA   = Clinical Trial Application/Authorisation
DMC   = Data Monitoring Committee
EudraCT = The European Union Drug Regulating Authorities Clinical Trials (database)
GCP   = Good Clinical Practice
GLP   = Good Laboratory Practice
GMP   = Good Manufacturing Practice
HA   = Health Authority
IB   = Investigator's Brochure
ICH   = International Conference on Harmonization
IEC   = Independent Ethics Committee
IMP   = Investigational medicinal product
IMPD = Investigational medicinal product dossier
SAE   = Serious adverse events
SAR   = Serious adverse reaction
SCV   = Site closure visit
SDV   = Source data verification
SIV   = Site initiation visit
SmPC = Summary of Product Characteristics
SMV   = Site monitoring visit
SOP   = Standard operating procedure
SUSAR = Serious unexpected suspected adverse reaction
TMF   = Trial Master File

Glossary

Adverse Drug Reaction (ADR), synonyms: Adverse reaction, suspected adverse (drug) reaction

[ICH GCP 1.1] In the pre-approval clinical experience with a new medicinal product or its new usages, particularly as the therapeutic dose(s) may not be established, all noxious and unintended responses to the medicinal product related to any dose should be considered adverse drug reactions. The phrase 'response to a medicinal product' means that a causal relationship between the medicinal (investigational) product and the adverse event is at least a reasonable possibility, i.e. the relationship cannot be ruled out. Regarding marketed medicinal products: a response to a drug that is noxious and unintended, and which occurs at doses normally used in man for prophylaxis, diagnosis or therapy of diseases, or for modification of physiological function.

Adverse Event (AE), synonym: Adverse experience

Any untoward medical occurrence in a patient or clinical trial subject administered a medicinal product and which does not necessarily have to have a causal relationship with this treatment. An adverse event can therefore be any unfavourable and unintended sign (including an abnormal laboratory finding), e.g. symptom or disease temporally associated with the use of a medicinal (investigational) product, whether or not related to the medicinal (investigational) product.

Adverse Event Onset

Earliest date, on which signs or symptoms of the event were noted, *after* drug therapy was started, not the date the diagnosis was made (e.g. dyspepsia and later diagnosis of ulcer). If the symptoms were present prior to drug start date, the drug start date becomes the event onset date (worsening of already existing disease). In clinical studies, the event onset date may precede the date on which the event became serious.

Age Groups

Neonate = Birth <1 month; Infant = ≥1 month to <2 years; Child = ≥2 to <12 years; Adolescent = ≥12 to <18 years; Adult = ≥18 to <65 years; Elderly = ≥65 years.

Applicable Regulatory Requirements

[ICH GCP 1.4] Any law(s) and regulation(s) addressing the conduct of clinical trials of investigational products.

Approval (in relation to Institutional Review Boards [IRBs])

[ICH GCP 1.5] The affirmative decision of the IRB that the clinical trial has been reviewed and may be conducted at the institution site within the constraints set forth by the IRB, the institution, Good Clinical Practice (GCP), and the applicable regulatory requirements.

Archiving

The process by which paper and electronic data and associated clinical trial documentation produced during the design, processing and analysis of a trial are securely stored, carefully catalogued, and readily available for regulatory inspection or other authorized access.

Assent

An affirmative decision from a clinical trial subject who is unable to give full consent (e.g. a vulnerable subject).

Audit

[ICH GCP 1.6] A systematic and independent examination of trial-related activities and documents to determine whether the evaluated trial-related activities were conducted, and the data were recorded, analyzed and accurately reported according to the protocol, sponsor's Standard Operating Procedures, Good Clinical Practice, and the applicable regulatory requirement(s).

Audit Certificate

[ICH GCP 1.7] A declaration of confirmation by the auditor that an audit has taken place.

Audit Report

[ICH GCP 1.8] A written evaluation by the sponsor's auditor of the results of the audit.

Audit Trail

[ICH GCP 1.9] Documentation that allows reconstruction of the course of events.

Autoencoder

A suite of computer programs used to assign codes to textual data recorded in Case Report Forms (e.g. adverse events, concomitant medications) to aid categorization of data for the purpose of analysis.

Bar Code

A bar code (also barcode) is an optical machine-readable representation of data. Originally, bar codes represent data in the widths (lines) and the spacing of parallel lines and may be referred to as linear or 1-dimensional (1D) barcodes or symbologies. They also come in patterns of squares, dots, hexagons and other geometric patterns within images termed 2D (2-dimensional) matrix codes or symbologies.

Baseline Assessments

The assessments performed on clinical trial subjects before any investigational product is administered.

Batch

A specific quantity or lot of a test item or reference item produced during a defined cycle of manufacture in such a way that it could be expected to be of a uniform character and should be designated as such.

Batch Number

A distinctive combination of numbers and/or letters which uniquely identifies a batch on the labels, its batch records and corresponding certificates of analysis, etc.

Benefit/Risk Ratio

An assessment of the expected benefits of an investigational product versus the potential risks from use of the product.

Bioavailability Study

A clinical trial to evaluate the rate and the extent to which an investigational product or new drug formulation reaches the systemic circulation.

Blinding/Masking

[ICH GCP 1.10] A procedure in which one or more parties to the trial are kept unaware of the treatment assignment(s). Single-blinding usually refers to the subject(s) being unaware, and double-blinding usually refers to the subject(s), investigator(s), monitor, and, in some cases, data analyst(s), being unaware of the treatment assignment(s).

Blister

A package consisting of a clear plastic overlay affixed to a cardboard backing for protecting and displaying a product.

Block Size

The organization of a randomization code into equal blocks of sequential numbers, to ensure that an approximately equal number of trial subjects within each clinical trial site receive each of the investigational products, even if individual investigators do not recruit their full quota of subjects. See also Randomization Code.

Brand Name

The trade name of a marketed medicinal product.

CADP

All data collected electronically in conjunction with a trial of Phase 1 up to 4 are collected through this computerized system supported by Biometry. Besides the facilities to track information supporting the study conduct and the capabilities to capture study subject-related data, many more functions are imbedded into this system. The individual capabilities are adaptable for each study and project and therefore a close collaboration with the study team is necessary to customize the system to the particular needs of a study or project.

Case Report Form (CRF)

[ICH GCP 1.11] A printed, optical, or electronic document designed to record all of the protocol-required information to be reported to the sponsor on each trial subject.

Causality

The relationship of an adverse event to the use of an investigational product.

Central Laboratory

A laboratory that analyses samples from a number of clinical trial sites in a multicentre trial. Samples are analyzed centrally to ensure consistency in methodology across sites.

Centralized Procedure

A centralized European Community regulatory procedure for the authorization of medicinal products, for which there is a single application, a single evaluation and a single authorization allowing direct access to the single market of the Community.

Certificate of Analysis (COA)

A document relating specifically to the result of testing a representative sample drawn from the batch of material to be delivered.

CIOMS I Form

An international regulatory reporting form developed by the Council for International Organizations of Medical Sciences (CIOMS) for the submission of individual case safety reports.

Clean Database

A clinical trial database from which errors have been eliminated.

Clinical Data Management (Department)

Department responsible for processing and validating clinical trial data, following retrieval of data from the trial site through to the final statistical analysis, according to the requirements of the sponsor's Standard Operating Procedures, Good Clinical Practice, and the applicable regulatory requirements.

Clinical Development Plan

A document produced by the sponsor detailing the clinical development program for an investigational product, including, but not limited to, details of the organization's business plan, individual clinical trials, timelines, milestones, responsibilities, budget and key decision points.

Clinical Significance

A clinically significant change is any change in a subject's clinical condition (which may or may not be due to treatment) that is regarded by the investigator as important. Changes that are statistically significant are not necessarily clinically significant.

Clinical Trial Database

Structured, tabular storage of all subject data from a clinical trial in a format that allows computerized processing and analysis.

Clinical Trial/Investigational Site

The location(s) where clinical trial-related activities are actually conducted (i.e. where protocol-related activities involve clinical trial subjects).

Clinical Trial Materials/Supplies

The complete set of supplies provided by the sponsor to investigators to enable them to complete a clinical trial. (Clinical trial materials may include but are not limited to: investigational product(s), case report forms, laboratory kits and postal packs, investigator's trial site file, etc.).

Clinical Trial/Study

[ICH GCP 1.12] Any investigation in human subjects intended to discover or verify the clinical, pharmacological and/or other pharmacodynamic effects of an investigational product(s), and/or to identify any adverse reactions to an investigational product(s), and/or to study absorption, distribution, metabolism, and excretion of an investigational product(s) with the object of ascertaining its safety and/or efficacy. The terms 'clinical trial' and 'clinical study' are synonymous.

Clinical Trial/Study Report

[ICH GCP 1.13] A written description of a trial/study of any therapeutic, prophylactic, or diagnostic agent conducted in human subjects, in which the clinical and statistical description, presentations, and analyses are fully integrated into a single report.

Clinical Trial Variables

The parameters observed, measured or assessed during the course of a clinical trial.

Closed Database

The status of a clinical trial database after all quality control and data validation procedures have been performed and which is a complete and accurate record of all data collected during the clinical trial.

Close Out/Close Down Visit

A visit to a clinical trial site by the sponsor's nominated representative(s) in order to reconcile and terminate all trial-related activities at that site.

Cohort

A cohort is a group of persons who experience a certain event in a specified period of time. For example, the birth cohort of 1985 would be the people born in that year.

Coinvestigator (Subinvestigator)

[ICH GCP 1.56] Any individual member of the clinical trial team designated and supervised by the investigator at a trial site to perform critical trial-related procedures and/or to make important trial-related decisions (e.g. associates, residents, research fellows).

Committee for Medicinal Products for Human Use (CHMP)

The Committee for Medicinal Products for Human Use (CHMP) is responsible for preparing the Agency's opinions on all questions concerning medicinal products for human use, in accordance with Regulation (EC) No 726/2004.

Comparative Study

A clinical trial in which one product is compared against another (e.g. standard therapy, placebo, other investigational product).

Comparator (Product)

[ICH GCP 1.14] An investigational or marketed product (i.e. active control), or placebo, used as a reference in a clinical trial.

Compassionate Use
An emergency Investigational New Drug procedure that allows for the clinical use of an unlicensed product in an individual patient.

Competent Authorities
Regulatory Authorities with the capacity to authorize and inspect clinical trials.

Common Technical Document (CTD)
A common organization for the contents of a marketing or licensing application, designed to be used across the ICH regions.

Compliance (in relation to Clinical Trials)
Adherence on the part of either the sponsor or the clinical trial site to all clinical trial-related requirements, applicable Standard Operating Procedures, Good Clinical Practice and the applicable regulatory requirements.

Compliance (in relation to the Subject)
Adherence to all the trial-related requirements, Good Clinical Practice requirements, and the applicable regulatory requirements.

Concurrent/Concomitant Medication
Medication taken by the subject during the course of a clinical trial, in addition to the investigational product(s).

Concurrent/Concomitant Treatment
Treatment undertaken by the subject during the course of a clinical trial, in addition to the investigational product(s) and protocol-related procedures.

Confidence Interval
A range of values within which the population mean is likely to lie. A 95% confidence interval means that there is a 95% probability that the true population mean will lie somewhere between the upper and lower confidence limits.

Confidentiality
[ICH GCP 1.16] Prevention of disclosure, other than to authorized individuals, of a sponsor's proprietary information or of a subject's personal data.

Consumer
A person who is not a Healthcare Professional such as patient, lawyer, friend or relative/parents/children of the patient.

Continuation Protocol
A protocol that allows a subject to continue taking investigational product after the completion of the original clinical trial assessments, through participation in an extended phase of the trial, during which a different or reduced set of parameters may be evaluated.

Contract

[ICH GCP 1.17] A written, dated and signed agreement between two or more involved parties that sets out any arrangements on delegation and distribution of tasks and obligations and, if appropriate, on financial matters. The protocol may serve as the basis of a contract.

Contract Research Organization (CRO)

[ICH GCP 1.20] A person or an organization (e.g. commercial, academic, other) contracted by the sponsor to perform one or more of a sponsor's trial-related duties and functions.

Control Group

The cohort of subjects in a comparative clinical trial that receives the comparator product (e.g. placebo, alternative medication).

Controlled Study

A clinical trial that includes a control group.

Coordinating Investigator

[ICH GCP 1.19] An investigator assigned the responsibility for the coordination of investigators at different centres participating in a multicentre trial.

Coordinating (Steering) Committee

A committee acting on behalf of the sponsor to coordinate the conduct of a multicentre clinical trial.

Core Informed Consent Form (CICF)

Model of subject/patient information leaflet and informed consent form (see individual terms) that is provided with each protocol. It will be modified for each country/study site according to local requirements.

Cost/Benefit Analysis

An analysis to quantify in monetary terms the benefits associated with the use of an investigational product.

Critical Path

The shortest time from planning the clinical trial to the final report, designed to allow certain tasks to be conducted in parallel wherever feasible.

Cross-Over Study

A clinical trial in which subjects receive each of the treatments under test in a sequential manner, usually in random order. Each subject acts as his/her own control.

Data

A data value is an observation or measurement that is recorded in a case report form. A collection of data values is referred to as the plural form 'data'. (The term 'data value' may refer to textual as well as numerical data.)

Database Audit Trail

Documentation or electronic metadata that tracks all data entry and changes to a clinical trial database.

Database Closure/Lock/Release

The point at which the database is declared clean (i.e. all errors have been reconciled and no additional data remain to be entered) and available for statistical analysis.

Database Management Systems

A system developed to track, manage and process clinical trial data.

Database Set Up

The process by which the clinical trial database is designed to aid data entry and analysis of the data.

Database Structure

The design, format and organization of computerized storage of clinical trial data.

Data Collection

Data collected by an investigator during the course of a clinical trial and recorded in the case report form.

Data Entry Screens

The graphic user interface designed to aid data entry into the clinical trial database. Data entry screens will often mimic the format of data fields in the case report form.

Data Handling

The procedures by which clinical trial data are processed, from initial recording in a case report form, through to a validated, clean and locked database.

Data Handling Report

A clear, concise and unambiguous description of the procedures by which clinical trial data were processed.

Data Listings

A report listing all clinical trial data values entered into the database.

Data Lock Point

The date designated as the cut-off date for the data to be included in a particular safety update such as the Periodic Safety Update Report (PSUR). On this date, the data available to the author of the safety report is extracted for review and stored.

Data Management Plan

A document reflecting the current status of data management-related activities in relation to a particular clinical study. The scope of Data Management is: to deliver a computerized system to support the tracking; to carry out data capture and data cleaning of patient data (and necessary context information) collected during a clinical study; to support the clinical team in setting up various documents specifying how the above activities should be defined and supported; to deliver to the clinical team data listings, summaries and graphical representations supporting the data cleaning process.

Data Query

A query raised about a single data value that requires resolution.

Data Query Resolution

The clarification of a data value following a query.

Data Query Resolution Form (Data Clarification Form)

A form used to track the resolution of data queries.

Data Set

A set of relational variables/assessments that are grouped together for analysis and reporting purposes.

Data Sheet

Official document describing information on the presentation of a licensed medicinal product, its recommended dose, indications, contraindications, and any precautions associated with its use. See also Summary of Product Characteristics (SmPC).

Data Validation

The process of data checking that ensures that data contained in the clinical trial database are complete, legible, logical, consistent and within an expected range.

Dechallenge

A reduction in dosage or discontinuation of a drug in response to an adverse event.

Declaration of Helsinki

The World Medical Association's statement (universally accepted as the international standard) of ethical principles to provide guidance to physicians and other participants in medical research involving human subjects.

Demographic Data

The characteristics of the clinical trial subjects (e.g. sex, age, age at onset of disease, family history of disease, etc.).

Diary Cards

Cards given to clinical trial subjects for recording specified information at regular intervals (e.g. daily record of symptoms, reminder to take dosages at the appropriate times).

Direct Access

[ICH GCP 1.21] Permission to examine, analyze, verify and reproduce any records and reports that are important to the evaluation of a clinical trial. Any party (e.g. domestic and foreign regulatory authorities, sponsors, monitors and auditors) with direct access should take all reasonable precautions within the constraints of the applicable regulatory requirement(s) to maintain the confidentiality of subjects' identities and sponsor's proprietary information.

Distributor

A business which supplies clinical trial materials (investigational product, emergency envelopes, import licenses, etc.) either to other distributors or directly to the end user.

Document

Recorded information which can be treated as a unit. A document may be edited and can exist in physical or electronic form.

Documented Procedures

Written procedures relating to the conduct of a clinical trial (including, but not limited to: Good Clinical Practice, Standard Operating Procedures, working practices, and trial-specific guidelines and procedures).

Dose Response Curve

A curve shown on a graph where dose is plotted on the x-axis and response is plotted on the y-axis.

Dosing Schedule

The length of treatment, dose amount and frequency of dose assigned to a clinical trial subject.

Double-Blind Study

A clinical trial in which relevant parties (normally the subject and the investigator) are unaware of the identity of the treatment assigned.

Double Data Entry

The process by which clinical trial data are entered into a database twice, by independent data entry officers, in order to compare entries and reduce the number of errors.

Double-Dummy

A technique enabling two drugs with different dose forms (e.g. tablets and capsules) to be compared in a double-blind manner, by the provision of placebo matching both dose forms.

Drop Out

A clinical trial subject who withdraws voluntarily from the study prematurely. See also Withdrawals.

Drug Abuse

Persistent or sporadic intentional excessive use of a drug, inconsistent with, or unrelated to, the recommendations of the product information or acceptable medical practice.

Drug Accountability

A record of the supply, use and disposal of all investigational product throughout the duration of a clinical trial.

Drug-Drug Interaction

A pharmacological or clinical response to the administration of a drug combination (or one shortly after another) different from that anticipated from the known effects of the two agents when given individually.

Drug Resistance

The reduction in therapeutic benefit in a subject who has been exposed to a medicinal product continuously (e.g. due to the emergence of resistant virus in the treatment of the human immunodeficiency virus).

Efficacy

The ability of an investigational product to produce the purported beneficial effects of treatment.

Efficacy Data

Data values collected to aid evaluation of any beneficial effects of the investigational product.

Electronic Common Technical Document

A format that allows the electronic transfer of the Common Technical Document files, including metadata, from a sponsor to a health authority.

Electronic Data Capture (EDC)

A method of collecting clinical trial data values (e.g. electronic case report form data, diary card data, scans, laboratory data) directly into electronic format.

Electronic Document Management System (EDMS)

An electronic system that preserves content, structure and context of the electronic records, and that has the capability to provide review and approval procedures, and audit trails.

Eligible Subject

A clinical trial subject who meets all the inclusion and none of the exclusion criteria described in a clinical trial protocol. An eligible subject is not necessarily one who has given consent.

Endpoint

Overall outcome that the protocol is designed to evaluate. Common endpoints are severe toxicity, disease progression, or death.

Entered/Enrolled Subject

A subject who has given written consent to participate in a clinical trial, is allocated a unique subject study number, and undergoes the first protocol-related assessment.

Essential Documentation

[ICH GCP 1.23] Documents which individually and collectively permit evaluation of the conduct of a clinical trial and the quality of the data produced. Essential Documents are listed in ICH GCP Section 8.0.

European Medicines Agency (EMA)

The European Union body headquartered in London with responsibility for the protection and promotion of public and animal health, through the evaluation and supervision of medicines for human and veterinary use.

European Qualified Person for Pharmacovigilance (EUQP PV)
The Marketing Authorization Holder should have permanently and continuously at his disposal a Qualified Person Responsible for Pharmacovigilance, residing in the EU.

EudraCT (European Union Drug Regulating Authorities Clinical Trials) Number
Each clinical trial with at least one site in the European Union receives this unique number for identification. The EudraCT Number must be included on all Clinical Trial Applications within the European Community and as needed on other documents relating to the trials (e.g. SUSAR reports).

Evaluable Subject
A subject entered into a clinical trial in accordance with the trial protocol and who has complied within the stipulated limits for adherence to investigational product and the required study assessments.

Exclusion Criteria
A list of criteria identified in the clinical trial protocol, any one of which should exclude the subject from participating in the trial.

FDA 1571
A form required by the FDA when an Investigational New Drug submission is filed.

FDA 1572
Statement of Investigator form, which includes details of the investigator's educational background, clinical appointments and expertise, required by the FDA for all investigators taking part in a clinical trial conducted under FDA regulations.

Financial Agreement
A formal document or letter laying down the financial arrangements between the sponsor and the investigator.

Financial Disclosure Statement
A document required by the FDA to clarify any financial interest on the part of the investigator and co investigators, in the sponsor's organization, investigational product or other financial concern which might unduly influence their participation in a clinical trial.

First-in-Man Study
The first clinical trial of a new chemical entity in human subjects.

First Patient/Subject, First Visit (FP/SFV)
The date on which the first visit of the first patient/subject in a clinical trial was carried out, as defined in the protocol.

Follow-up Assessment
A further consultation between the clinical trial subject and the investigator, to evaluate the continued efficacy and safety of an investigational product.

Food and Drug Administration (FDA)
The US federal government body with the authority to ensure that all drugs on the US market are safe and effective.

Fraud
The deliberate falsification or forgery of clinical trial data.

Generic Name
The name given to a chemical compound that can be used by more than one manufacturer of a medicinal product.

Good Clinical Practice (GCP)
[ICH GCP 1.24] A standard for the design, conduct, performance, monitoring, auditing, recording, analyses and reporting of clinical trials that provides assurance that the data and reported results are credible and accurate, and that the rights, integrity and confidentiality of the trial subjects are protected.

Good Laboratory Practice (GLP)
Good Laboratory Practice (GLP) is a quality system concerned with the organizational process and the conditions under which non-clinical health and environmental safety studies are planned, performed, monitored, recorded, archived and reported.

Good Manufacturing Practice (GMP)
A standard to ensure that pharmaceutical products are consistently manufactured and controlled to the quality appropriate to the intended use.

Good Pharmacovigilance Practice (GPvP)
A concept encompassing standards for the conduct performance, monitoring, auditing, recording, analysis and reporting of pharmacovigilance data that provides assurance that the recorded data and reported information are credible and accurate and that the rights, integrity and confidentiality of patients and reporters are protected by all parties involved.

Half-Life (of drugs)
The time taken for the body to eliminate half the drug circulating in the blood. The time taken for the plasma concentration to fall by 50% when absorption and distribution of the drug within the body are complete.

Healthcare Professional
For the purpose of reporting suspected adverse reactions, Healthcare Professionals are defined as medically qualified persons, such as physicians, pharmacists, nurses and coroners.

Historical Control
Comparison of a clinical trial treatment group with historical data from past experience, often used to compare an outcome of a new treatment with the natural course of the clinical condition under test (e.g. when untreated, or when treated with previously available therapy).

iHUB

The business unit responsible for the operation and maintenance of iTRACK, a well-known clinical trial management system.

Impartial Witness

[ICH GCP 1.26] A person, who is independent of the trial, who cannot be unfairly influenced by people involved with the trial, who attends the informed consent process if the subject or the subject's legally acceptable representative cannot read, and who reads the informed consent form and any other written information supplied to the subject.

Inclusion/Exclusion Criteria

The medical or social standards determining whether a person may or may not be allowed to enter a clinical trial. These criteria are based on such factors as age, gender, the type and stage of a disease, previous treatment history, and other medical conditions. It is important to note that inclusion and exclusion criteria are not used to reject people personally, but rather to identify appropriate participants and keep them safe.

Indemnification/Indemnity

Insurance cover provided by a sponsor to an investigator (and, if applicable, to the clinical trial site and/or the local health authority) in the event of an untoward occurrence that may result in a clinical trial subject taking legal action against the doctor or health authority, and where there is no evidence of negligence on the part of the doctor or health authority.

Independent Data Monitoring Committee (IDMC)/Data and Safety Monitoring Board (DSMB)

[ICH GCP 1.25] An independent data monitoring committee that may be established by the sponsor to assess, at intervals, the progress of a clinical trial, the safety data, and the critical efficacy endpoints, and to recommend to the sponsor whether to continue, modify or stop the trial.

Independent Ethics Committee (IEC)

[ICH GCP 1.27] An independent body (an institutional, regional, national, or supranational review board or committee), constituted of medical/scientific professionals and non-medical/non-scientific members. The responsibility of the IEC is to ensure the protection of the rights, safety and well-being of human subjects involved in a trial, and to provide public assurance of that protection by, among other things, reviewing and approving/providing favourable opinion on the trial protocol, the suitability of the investigator(s), facilities, and the methods and material to be used in obtaining and documenting informed consent of the trial subjects. The legal status, composition, function, operations and regulatory requirements pertaining to Independent Ethics Committees may differ among countries, but should allow the Independent Ethics Committee to act in agreement with GCP as described in the ICH guideline.

Individual Case Safety Report (ICSR), synonym: Safety Report

A document providing the most complete information related to an individual case at a certain point of time. An individual case is the information provided by a primary source to describe suspected adverse reaction(s) related to the administration of one or more medicinal products to an individual Patient at a particular point of time.

Ineligible Subjects

Subjects who do not meet the inclusion criteria and/or do meet an exclusion criterion laid down in a clinical trial protocol.

Informed Consent

[ICH GCP 1.28] A process by which a subject voluntarily confirms his or her willingness to participate in a particular clinical trial, after having been informed of all aspects of the trial that are relevant to the subject's decision to participate. Informed consent is documented by means of a written, signed and dated informed consent form.

Initiation Visit

The visit by the sponsor's monitor to the clinical trial site at the point at which all essential approvals and documents are in place and the site is ready for delivery of all clinical trial materials necessary to commence the trial.

Inspection

[ICH GCP 1.29] The act, by a Regulatory Authority(ies), of conducting an official review of documents, facilities, records, and any other resources that are deemed by the Authority(ies) to be related to the clinical trial and that may be located at the site of the trial, at the sponsor and/or contract research organization's) facilities, or at other establishments deemed appropriate by the Regulatory Authority(ies).

Institution (Medical)

Any public or private entity, agency, or medical or dental facility where clinical trials are conducted.

Institutional Review Board (IRB)

[ICH GCP 1.31] An independent body constituted of medical, scientific and non-scientific members, whose responsibility it is to ensure the protection of the rights, safety and well-being of human subjects involved in a trial by, among other things, reviewing, approving, and providing continuing review of the trial, of protocols and amendments, and of the methods and material to be used in obtaining and documenting informed consent of the trial subjects.

Integrity of Data

The accuracy and validity of data.

Intention-to-Treat Analysis

Statistical analysis performed on all data collected during a clinical trial, irrespective of the subjects' suitability or compliance with the trial protocol. The intention-to-treat population includes all subjects for whom there are any data, regardless of their eligibility or evaluability.

Interim Analysis

A planned analysis, at a predetermined time, performed before all subjects have completed a clinical trial.

Interim Clinical Trial/Study Report

[ICH GCP 1.32] A report of intermediate results and their evaluation based on analyses performed during the course of a clinical trial.

Internal Audit

An audit by an employee of the organization being audited.

International Birth Date (IBD)

The date of the first marketing authorization for a medicinal product granted to the Marketing Authorization Holder in any country in the world.

International Conference on Harmonization (ICH)

International Conference on Harmonization (of Technical Requirements for Registration of Pharmaceuticals for Human Use).

Invasive Procedure

Any procedure that involves the insertion of a piece of equipment or apparatus into a subject.

Investigational Medicinal Product (IMP)

See Investigational Product. Investigational Medicinal Product is the nomenclature used by the European Medicines Agency and the Committee for Medicinal Products for Human Use.

Investigational Medicinal Product Dossier (IMPD)

The Investigational Medicinal Product Dossier (IMPD) is the basis for approval of clinical trials by the competent authorities in the EU. The IMPD includes summaries of information related to the quality, manufacture and control of the Investigational Medicinal Product, data from non-clinical studies and from its clinical use. An overall risk-benefit assessment, critical analyses of the non-clinical and clinical data in relation to the potential risks and benefits of the proposed study have to be part of the IMPD. In certain situations, e.g. where the Investigational Medicinal Product has already been authorized as a medicinal product in one of the EU Member States or where clinical studies with the IMP have already been approved by a Member State, a simplified IMPD will be sufficient.

Investigational New Drug (IND) Application

Official procedure for the notification to the United States Food and Drug Administration of the intention to conduct a clinical trial.

Investigational Product

[ICH GCP 1.33] A pharmaceutical form of an active ingredient or placebo being tested or used as a reference in a clinical trial, including a product with a Marketing Authorization when used or assembled (formulated or packaged) in a way different from the approved form, or when used for an unapproved indication, or when used to gain further information about an approved use. (The term Investigational Product may also apply to a medical device.)

Investigator

[ICH GCP 1.34] A person responsible for the conduct of the clinical trial at a trial site. If a trial is conducted by a team of individuals at a trial site, the investigator is the responsible leader of the team and may be called the principal investigator (see also Principal Investigator and Coinvestigator/Subinvestigator).

Investigator Agreement

A formal document signed by the investigator which describes his or her role, responsibilities and obligations in conducting a clinical trial in accordance with the principles of Good Clinical Practice.

Investigator Meeting

A meeting held between the sponsor and the investigators and/or coinvestigators participating in a clinical trial, whether pre-study, during the trial and/or after the trial, with the purpose of exchanging information relevant to the investigational product(s) and the conduct of the trial, to motivate investigators, and to report on progress with the trial.

Investigator's Brochure (IB)

[ICH GCP 1.36] Collection of clinical and non-clinical data in human subjects relevant to the study of investigational drug (including known AEs).

Investigator Trial Site File/Trial File

All documentation kept at the trial site pertaining to a clinical trial, including, but not limited to, copies of case report forms, electronic data, protocol, Investigator's Brochure and other essential written documentation related to the trial, approvals, correspondence and a copy of the final clinical trial report.

Labelling

Process of identifying a product including the following information, as appropriate: name, active ingredient(s): type and amount, batch number, expiry date, special storage conditions or handling precautions, directions for use, warnings, and precautions; names and addresses of the manufacturer and/or the supplier.

Laboratory Data

Data obtained from laboratory analysis of a biological sample.

Laboratory Normal Range/Reference Range

A range of laboratory values, between an upper and a lower limit specific to each parameter and to the laboratory, in which data from a 'normal' population of subjects would be expected to lie.

Last Patient/Subject, Last Visit (LP/SLV)

Either the date of the last patient visit of the last patient to complete the study, or the date at which the last data point from the last patient, which was required for statistical analysis (i.e. key safety and efficacy results for decision making), was received, whichever is the later date.

Legally Acceptable Representative

[ICH GCP 1.37] An individual or juridical or other body authorized under applicable law to consent, on behalf of a prospective subject, to the subject's participation in the clinical trial.

Life-Threatening

Patient was at immediate risk of death from an adverse event according to reporter. It does not refer to an event that hypothetically might have caused death, had it been more severe.

Loading Dose

A first dose of drug, larger than subsequent doses, to ensure that drug levels in the blood reach therapeutic levels quickly.

Local Laboratory

A local facility that provides data from the laboratory analysis of biological samples.

Local Studies

Clinical trials conducted on a national basis, often by a local subsidiary of a company, to support the marketing of a product. Local studies are typically (but are not limited to) Phase 4 clinical trials (see also Medical Marketing Studies).

Logging (of Case Report Forms [CRFs])

The process for recording that a Case Report Form has been collected from a clinical trial site, and for tracking its whereabouts within the sponsor's facilities thereafter.

Marketing Authorization (Product License, Registration Certificate)

A legal document issued by the competent drug regulatory authority that establishes the detailed composition and formulation of the product and the pharmacopoeial or other recognized specifications of its ingredients and of the final product itself, and includes details of packaging, labelling and shelf-life.
Marketing authorization, or product license, which enables the manufacturer to market a medicinal product for the approved indications.

Marketing Authorization Application (MAA)

Submission of all the relevant nonclinical and clinical data pertaining to an investigational product to a Regulatory Authority(ies) in order to apply for a Marketing Authorization Approval.

Marketing Authorization Holder (MAH)

Those who market, lease and/or grant the products (which are manufactured or imported).

Master Schedule

A compilation of information to assist in the assessment of workload and for the tracking of studies at a test facility (GLP).

Mean

A measure of the average of a sample of observations formed by summing the values and dividing by the number of observations. The mean is the sum of the observations divided by the number of observations.

Medical Marketing Studies

Phase 4 studies conducted to provide clinical trial data for use by the marketing department to promote the product in the market place where the product has been granted a Marketing Authorization Approval.

MedDRA or Medical Dictionary for Regulatory Activities

A clinically validated international medical terminology used by regulatory authorities and the regulated biopharmaceutical industry throughout the entire regulatory process, from pre-marketing to post-marketing activities, and for data entry, retrieval, evaluation and presentation. In addition, it is the adverse event classification dictionary endorsed by the International Conference on Harmonization (ICH). MedDRA is used in the US, European Union, and Japan. Its use is currently mandated in Europe and Japan for safety reporting.

Median

A statistical value, determined by ordering a set of data from the smallest to the largest value. For data with an odd number of observations, the median is the value which lies at the centre of the list of ordered values. For data with an even number of observations, the median is the simple arithmetic mean of the two values in the centre of the list of observations.

Medicinal Product

Any product that may be given to a subject with the intention of producing therapeutic benefit.

Medicines and Healthcare Products Regulatory Agency (MHRA)

The UK Regulatory Authority responsible for approval of Clinical Trial Applications and Marketing Authorization Applications.

MedWatch

The FDA Safety Information and Adverse Event Reporting Program; for use by user-facilities, distributors and manufacturers for mandatory reporting.

MedWatch 3500A

FDA form for reporting drug experiences.

Member State

A country that is part of the European Union (EU).

Metadata

With regard to records management, information that describes objects and defines how they are managed through time. This includes the objects' properties, attributes, security, indexing, etc.

Monitor

A person nominated by the sponsor to oversee the progress of a clinical trial at a specific trial site(s), and to ensure that it is conducted, recorded, and reported in accordance with the protocol, Standard Operating Procedures, Good Clinical Practice, and the applicable regulatory requirements.

Monitoring

[ICH GCP 1.38] The act of overseeing the progress of a clinical trial, and of ensuring that it is conducted, recorded and reported in accordance with the protocol, Standard Operating Procedures, Good Clinical Practice, and the applicable regulatory requirement(s).

Monitoring Report

[ICH GCP 1.39] A written report from the monitor to the sponsor after each site visit and/or other trial-related communication, according to the sponsor's Standard Operating Procedures.

Monitoring Visit Log

A record, filed in the investigator's trial site file, signed and dated by all sponsor's nominated representatives visiting the trial site in connection with the clinical trial.

Multicentre Trial

A clinical trial conducted according to a single protocol but at more than one site. These sites may be across multiple countries.

Mutual Recognition Procedure

A European Union regulatory procedure aimed at facilitating access to a single market by relying upon the principle of mutual recognition. Thus a marketing authorization or the assessment in one Member State (the so-called reference Member State) ought, in principle, to be recognized by the competent authorities of the other Member States (the so-called concerned Member States), unless there are grounds for supposing that the authorization of the medicinal product concerned may present a potential serious risk to public health.

Named Patient Basis

The sole use of an unlicensed medicinal product in a specific, named patient, under the supervision of his or her physician (See also Compassionate Use).

New Chemical Entity

A new chemical compound, in development as a prescription medicine for the treatment or prophylaxis of a medical condition.

New Drug Application (NDA)

An application to the US Food and Drug Administration (FDA) for a license to market a new drug in the United States.

Nonclinical Health and Environmental Safety Study

An experiment or set of experiments in which a test item is examined under laboratory conditions or in the environment to obtain data on its properties and/or its safety, intended for submission to appropriate regulatory authorities.

Non-Clinical Study, synonym: Pre-Clinical Study

[ICH GCP 1.41] Biomedical studies not performed on human subjects.

Non-Comparative Study

A clinical trial in which no comparator product is used.

Non-Evaluable Subject

A subject whose clinical trial data cannot be included in the efficacy analyses.

Non-Interventional Trial

A study where the medicinal product(s) is (are) prescribed in the usual manner in accordance with the terms of the marketing authorization. The assignment of the patient to a particular therapeutic strategy is not decided in advance by a trial protocol but falls within current practice and the prescription of the medicine is clearly separated from the decision to include the patient in the study. No additional diagnostic or monitoring procedures shall be applied to the patients and epidemiological methods shall be used for the analysis of collected data.

Non-Pivotal Study

A clinical trial that is not a critical part of a Marketing Authorization Application but which may provide additional supportive data (See also Supportive Data).

Normal Range

See Laboratory Normal Range/Reference Range.

Notification

A procedure for informing Regulatory Authorities of a sponsor's intention to undertake a clinical trial.

Observational Studies

Studies in which the investigator does not control the therapy, but observes and evaluates the results of ongoing medical care. The study designs that are used are those that do not involve random allocation, namely case reports, case series, analyses of secular trends, case-control studies, and cohort studies.

Off-Label (Use of Drugs)

The use of a product other than that for which it has been granted a Marketing Authorization Application.

On-Line Validation

A series of validation checks conducted whilst data are being entered remotely.

Open Study

A clinical trial in which all parties are aware of the identity of the treatment given.

Opinion Leader

A leading expert on a particular subject at a local, national or international level, whose opinion on the subject is recognized and credible to others working within the same field of expertise.

Orphan Drug

A drug developed for the treatment of a rare condition or that is effective in a therapeutic area with only a small number of patients.

Over-the-Counter (OTC) Medicinal Product

A product that can be purchased by the general public in a pharmacy or supermarket.

Package Insert

A leaflet included with a proprietary medicine, giving prescribing information, contra-indications and precautions. See also Data Sheet and Summary of Product Characteristics (SmPC).

Parallel (Group) Study

A clinical trial in which two or more investigational products (including placebo) are compared in parallel, with subjects randomly allocated to each treatment group.

Patient/Subject Identifier (ID)

A unique identifier assigned by the investigator to each clinical trial subject, in addition to, or instead of, the subject study number, in lieu of the subject's name, in order to protect the subject's identity when the investigator reports adverse events and/or other trial-related data (see also Subject Study Number).

Patient/Subject Information Leaflet

Written information given to a subject during the informed consent process, describing all aspects of the clinical trial that is relevant to the subject's decision to participate (see also Informed Consent).

Patient/Subject Pack

A pack of investigational product intended and labelled for an individual subject.

Patient/Subject Screening Log

A log of all subjects who presented at a clinical trial site during the study recruitment period with the condition being investigated in a trial, irrespective of whether or not the subject subsequently consented to participate in the trial.

Periodic Safety Update Report (PSUR)

An update report, at defined time points after authorization, of the worldwide safety experience of a medicinal product. The PSUR is to be submitted to the (Co-)Rapporteurs, all Member States and to the European Medicines Agency (EMA). At these time points, the Marketing Authorization Holder is expected to provide succinct summary information together with a critical evaluation of the benefit/risk balance of the product in the light of new or changing post-authorization information. This evaluation should ascertain whether further investigations need to be carried out and whether changes should be made to the marketing authorization (e.g. to the product information).

Pharmacodynamics

The study of the action of drugs on the physiology of the body.

Pharmacoeconomics

The quantification of monetary savings made and of improvements in the quality of life for subjects treated with a pharmaceutical product or device.

Pharmacokinetics

The study of the rate of absorption, distribution and elimination of a drug and its metabolites from the body.

Pharmacology
The study of the biochemical and physiological effects of drugs on the body or on microorganisms or parasites within or on the body, and the mechanism of drug action and the relationship between drug concentration and effect.

Pharmacovigilance
The science and activities relating to the detection, assessment, understanding and prevention of adverse effects or any other medicinal product-related problem.

Phase
A defined activity or set of activities in the conduct of a study.

Phase 1 Study
A pharmacokinetic/pharmacodynamic study, or drug–drug interaction study, or study in special populations (e.g. elderly, Japanese, renal or liver dysfunction, etc.), or proof-of-concept study in healthy volunteers.

Phase 2a Study
An exploratory study (without a statistical hypothesis), or proof-of-concept study (with a statistical hypothesis), in patients.

Phase 2b Study
A dose-escalating, dose-ranging, dose-finding study.

Phase 3a Study
A study within a non-approved/labelled indication.

Phase 3b Study
A study within an approved indication, but with a different population (e.g. children versus adults) or with a different disease grading (e.g. severe versus mild to moderate), or with subset of patients not yet studied (without versus with metastasis), or with a new target claim (e.g. mortality versus symptomatic claim), etc.

Phase 4 Study
A study within approved labelling/claim: same indication and patient population.

Phase 5 Study
Survey or epidemiological study without administration of study drug.

Pilot Study
A clinical trial in a small group of subjects (e.g. to test feasibility of the methodology).

Pivotal Study
A clinical trial that forms a critical part of a Marketing Authorization Application.

Placebo
A pharmaceutical preparation (e.g. tablet, capsule, liquid) containing non-active ingredients and used as a comparator in placebo-controlled clinical trials.

Placebo-Controlled Study

A clinical trial comparing one or more treatments with a placebo.

Placebo Effect

The beneficial or adverse effects experienced by a subject who is unaware that his/her treatment is a placebo, due in part to a psychological belief that the treatment will be effective.

Post-Authorization Study

Any study conducted within the conditions laid down in the Summary of Product Characteristics and other conditions laid down for the marketing of the product or under normal conditions of use.

Post-Marketing Surveillance (PMS)

The monitoring of drug effects in a large number of subjects following the granting of a Marketing Authorization Application. PMS studies evaluate products as they are used in a wide spectrum of patients.

Power (of a Study)

The probability of detecting the expected difference between two treatments, if such a difference exists. A power of at least 80% is used to detect clinically-relevant differences for most controlled clinical trials.

Pre-Study Documentation

Essential documentation required prior to commencement of a clinical trial.

Pre-Study Visit

Visit(s) to the prospective clinical trial site by the sponsor's nominated representative(s) prior to commencement of a clinical trial at the trial site.

Primary Care Physician

A physician responsible for the general health of a subject (e.g. general practitioner [GP], family health doctor).

Principal Investigator

[GCP] The lead investigator at a clinical trial site and/or the lead investigator in a multi-centre trial.

Principal Investigator

[GLP] The individual who, for a multi-site study, acts on behalf of the Study Director and has defined responsibilities for delegated phases of the study.

Product Recall

A process for withdrawing or removing a pharmaceutical product from the pharmaceutical distribution chain because of defects in the product or complaints of serious adverse reactions to the product. The recall might be initiated by the manufacturer, importer, wholesaler, distributor or a responsible agency.

Prognostic Factors

A specific set of assessment parameters used to predict the course or outcome of the medical condition being studied.

Project-Specific Procedure (PSP)

A detailed account of activities to be performed during the conduct of related clinical trials undertaken within the context of a single project (e.g. concerning a common investigational compound). The PSP is a supplement to other project relevant documents such as the clinical trial protocol or Standard Operating Procedure. PSPs are created, maintained and managed by the issuing project team.

Prospective Study

A clinical trial in which subjects are recruited according to criteria laid down in a protocol (see also Retrospective Study).

Protocol

[ICH GCP 1.44] A document that describes the objective(s), design, methodology, statistical considerations, and organization of a clinical trial. The protocol usually also gives the background and rationale for the trial, but these could be provided in other protocol-referenced documents.

Protocol Amendment

[ICH GCP 1.45] A written description of a change(s) to or formal clarification of a protocol.

Protocol Deviation

A deviation from the criteria and methodology described in the protocol.

Protocol Violation

An event occurring within a clinical trial that is not in compliance with the protocol and for which an amendment has not been granted.

p-value (Significance Level)

The statistical probability of obtaining as big a difference between two treatments as that observed if in reality there is no difference. The smaller the p-value, the greater the likelihood that the effects of the two treatments are different. A p-value greater than 0.05 is not (statistically) significant).

Qualitative Data

Subjective data, categorized in descriptive terms, to which an absolute value cannot be assigned (e.g. mild, moderate, severe).

Quality Assurance (QA)

System of procedures, checks, audits and corrective actions to ensure that all testing, sampling, analysis, monitoring and other technical and reporting activities are of the highest achievable quality.

Quality Control (QC)

The supervision and control of all operations involved in a process usually involving sampling and inspection, in order to detect and correct systematic or excessively random variations in quality.

Quantitative Data

Data that can be assigned a numerical value.

Quorum (for Independent Ethics Committees)

The minimum number of members, as laid out in the independent ethics committee Standard Operating Procedures, that must be present at a meeting in order for the review of a protocol to be valid.

Randomization

[ICH GCP 1.48] The process of assigning trial subjects to treatment or control groups using an element of chance to determine the assignments in order to reduce bias.

Randomization Code

Documentation of the method for randomly assigning subjects to a treatment group in a clinical trial. The full randomization code is typically computer-generated in list form; individual subject codes are typically filed in separate sealed envelopes for emergency purposes (see also Block Size).

Randomized Study

A clinical trial in which subjects are randomly allocated to treatment groups according to a predetermined code.

Raw Data (GCP)

Records or certified copies of the original clinical and laboratory findings for subjects enrolled in a clinical trial (GCP). 'Raw data text' may also refer to a textual entry in a case report form prior to coding (e.g. raw text stating 'patient felt sick' might be coded as 'nausea' for analysis purposes) (see also Source Data/Source Documents).

Raw Data (GLP)

All original test facility records and documentation, or verified copies thereof, which are the result of the original observations and activities in a study. Raw data may also include, for example, photographs, microfilm or microfiche copies, computer readable media, dictated observations, recorded data from automated instruments, or any other data storage medium that has been recognized as capable of providing secure storage of information for a time period.

Rechallenge

A rechallenge is a resumption of the drug (regardless of dosage) after an interruption or an increase in a previously lowered dosage. It generally applies to the same route of administration. In order for an event to reappear on rechallenge (positive rechallenge), there must first be an improvement upon dechallenge (stopping or reducing dosage).

Reconciliation

Process of reconciling serious clinical trial adverse events in Argus (e.g. Oracle Argus Safety adverse events management system) with corresponding data in clinical trial databases.

Record

Information created, received and maintained in pursuance of legal obligations or in the transaction of business. A record may incorporate one or several objects and may be on any medium in any format. In addition to the content of the object(s), it should include contextual information and, if applicable, structural information (i.e. information which describes the components of the record). A key feature of a record is that it cannot be changed.

Records Management

The systematic control of documents and records from creation, for as long as they are retained.

Reference Item

Any article used to provide a basis for comparison with the test item.

Registry

An organized system for the collection, storage, retrieval, analysis and dissemination of information on individual persons exposed to a specific medical intervention who have either a particular disease, a condition (e.g. a risk factor) that predisposes [them] to the occurrence of a health-related event, or prior exposure to substances (or circumstances) known or suspected to cause adverse health effects.

Regulatory Approval

Approval by the relevant Regulatory Authority(ies), where required, for a clinical trial or clinical trial program to commence, or the granting of a Marketing Authorization Approval by a Regulatory Authority(ies).

Regulatory Authorities

[ICH GCP 1.49] are bodies having the power to regulate. In the ICH GCP guideline the expression Regulatory Authorities includes the Authorities that review submitted clinical data and those that conduct inspections. These bodies are sometimes referred to as Competent Authorities (see also Competent Authorities).

Remote Data Entry/Remote Site Entry

Data entered into the clinical trial database from a different location to that where the database is located: e.g. data may be entered at a trial site and downloaded by modem, or uploaded from a laptop computer brought into the data management department by the sponsor's monitor.

Rescue Medication

Permitted medication that may be provided to a clinical trial subject in the event that the investigational product does not adequately control the subject's condition.

Retrospective Study

A study where an investigator goes back in time through medical records to collate data from subjects according to defined criteria (with the subjects' consent).

Risk-Benefit Balance

An evaluation of the positive therapeutic effects of the medicinal products in relation to the risks (any risk relating to the quality, safety and efficacy of the medicinal products as regards patients' health or public health) [Article 1.28a. of Directive 2001/83/EC].

Risk Management System

A risk management system comprises of a set of pharmacovigilance activities and interventions designed to identify, prevent or minimize risks relating to medicinal products, including the assessment of the effectiveness of those interventions.

Run-in Period (of a Study)

A period in a clinical trial prior to administration of the investigational product e.g. to allow subjects to stabilize after withdrawal of previous medication so that baseline assessments can be made (see also Washout Period).

Safety Concern

An important identified risk, important potential risk or important missing information.

Safety Data

All data, including adverse events and laboratory parameters, collected to ascertain if the investigational product has any undesired effects with respect to the safety and well-being of study subjects.

Screening Assessments/Visits

Assessments to confirm that the subject is eligible to participate in a clinical trial, prior to receiving the investigational product. The subject must give consent before any screening assessments are performed for the purpose of the clinical trial.

Sequelae

After-effects of disease or injury, which prevent patient from carrying on a normal life over a prolonged period of time (e.g. insulin, partial gastrectomy), as compared to permanent disability (e.g. amputation, paralysis).

Serious Adverse Event (SAE) Criteria

[ICH GCP 1.50] Any untoward medical occurrence that at any dose: (1) results in death, (2) is life threatening (patient was at immediate risk of death at the time of the event in the opinion of the reporter), (3) requires inpatient hospitalization (at least 24 h) or prolongation of existing hospitalization, (4) results in persistent or significant disability/incapacity (substantial disruption in patient's ability to carry out normal daily activities over a long period of time), (5) requires intervention (FDA criterion) to prevent permanent impairment (e.g. emergency room treatment for allergic bronchospasms, excludes routine prescription drug treatment), or (6) was medically significant (in the judgment of the reporting or company physician, the event was serious, although not meeting the above criteria, e.g. convulsion).

Severity of Event

Not to be confused with 'serious'. (1) Mild: event may be noticeable to patient, does not influence daily activities, and usually does not require intervention. (2) Moderate: event may make patient uncomfortable; performance of daily activities may be influenced; intervention may be needed. (3) Severe: event may cause noticeable discomfort; usually interferes with daily activities; subject may not be able to continue in the study; treatment or intervention usually needed (may or may not be serious).

Short-Term Study

A study of a short duration with widely used, routine techniques.

Signal

Reported information on a possible causal relationship between an adverse event and a drug, the relationship being unknown or incompletely documented previously. Usually more than a single report is required to generate a signal, depending upon the seriousness of the event and the quality of the information.

Significance Level

The statistical method used to assess how strong the evidence is for a genuine difference in response to treatment.

Single-Blind Study

A clinical trial in which one party (e.g. either the subject or the investigator) is unaware of the treatment assigned to the subject.

SmartTrack

Drug Safety database that allows electronic collection of (and access to) all available documents pertaining to adverse event reports in one central system.

Source Data

[ICH GCP 1.51] All information in original records and certified copies of original records of clinical findings, observations, or other activities in a clinical trial necessary for the reconstruction and evaluation of the trial. Source data are contained in source documents (original records or certified copies) (see also Raw Data/Source Documents).

Source Documents

[ICH GCP 1.52] Original documents, data and records (e.g. hospital records; clinical and office charts; laboratory notes; memoranda; subjects' diaries or evaluation checklists; pharmacy dispensing records; recorded data from automated instruments; copies or transcriptions certified after verification as being accurate copies; microfiches; photographic negatives; microfilm or magnetic media; x-rays; subject files, and records kept at the pharmacy, laboratories and at other medico-technical departments involved in the clinical trial).

Source Document Verification (SDV)

Validation of the information recorded in the case report form by checking the recorded data against the original source documents at the clinical trial site.

Specimen

Any material derived from the test system for examination, analysis or retention (GLP).

Sponsor

[ICH GCP 1.53] An individual, company, institution or organization that takes responsibility for the initiation, management, and/or financing of a clinical trial or a non-clinical health and environmental safety study.

Sponsor-Investigator

[ICH GCP 1.54] An individual who both initiates and conducts, alone or with others, a clinical trial, and under whose immediate direction the investigational product is administered to, dispensed to, or used by a subject. The term does not include any person other than an individual (e.g. it does not include a corporation or agency). The obligations of a sponsor-investigator include both those of a sponsor and those of an investigator.

Spontaneous Reports

A communication to company, regulatory authority or other organization, that describes an adverse drug reaction in a patient given a drug, and which does not derive from a study. Spontaneous reports are provided without solicitation from: Health Professionals, Consumers, Attorneys, Sales Representatives, Regulatory Agencies, International/National Centres, or Licensee. A spontaneous report is medically confirmed if the case is reported by a health professional, regulatory agency, health centre, licensee, or the reporting consumer is also a physician.

Stability

The capacity of a drug product to remain within specifications established to ensure its identity, strength, quality and purity.

Standard Deviation

A statistical measure of the spread of the clinical trial data, based on averaging the distances of the data from the mean value. Standard deviation is the square root of variance (see also Variance).

Standard Error of the Mean

The precision with which a population mean is estimated, calculated by dividing the standard deviation by the square root of the number of subjects.

Standard Operating Procedure (SOP)

[ICH GCP 1.55] Detailed written instructions to achieve uniformity of the performance of a specific function.

Statistical Analysis

The analysis of clinical trial data using the methods and techniques laid down in the protocol and Statistical Analysis Plan (SAP).

Statistical Analysis Plan (SAP)

A document that describes the planned data analyses to be undertaken using data collected in a clinical trial, the timing of the analyses and the format for presentation and reporting of the results.

Steering Committee

A committee acting on behalf of the sponsor to coordinate the conduct of a multicentre clinical trial.

Stratification

The categorization of the clinical trial subject population into strata, in order to ensure that when the randomization code is implemented, subjects fulfilling the criteria of each stratum are evenly distributed between treatment groups.

Study Completion Date (GLP)

The date the Study Director signed the final report.

Subinvestigator

[ICH GCP 1.56] Any individual member of the clinical trial team designated and supervised by the investigator at a trial site to perform critical trial-related procedures and/or to make important trial-related decisions (e.g. associates, residents, research fellows). See also Coinvestigator, Investigator.

Subject Identification Code

A unique identifier assigned by the investigator to each trial subject, to protect the subject's identity and used in lieu of the subject's name when the investigator reports adverse events and/or other trial-related data.

Subject Identification (ID) Log

A confidential list of subject names assigned a subject study number, filed in the investigator's trial site file, to enable identification of subjects after a clinical trial for purposes of continued well-being of the subjects, and in order to verify that the subjects enrolled in a clinical trial actually existed.

Subject Identifier

See Patient/Subject Identifier.

Subjective Measurement/Parameter

A measurement that depends mainly on individual judgment or interpretation.

Subject Screening Log

A log of all subjects who presented at a clinical trial site during the study recruitment period with the medical condition under test, irrespective or whether or not the individual subjects listed gave their consent to participate in the trial.

Subject Study Number

A unique number assigned by the investigator to each clinical trial subject who has given consent to participate in the clinical trial, according to a predetermined system, such as a sequential randomization code, used to protect the subject's identity and as a reference on all clinical trial-related correspondence, case report forms and other documentation concerning that subject (see also Patient/Subject Identifier).

Subject/Trial Subject

[ICH GCP 1.57] An individual who participates in a clinical trial, either as a recipient of the investigational product(s) or as a control.

Summary of Product Characteristics (SmPC)

The summary of the product characteristics of an approved drug, produced by the Marketing Authorization Holder and setting out the details required by Article 11 of EU Directive 2001/83/EC, approved in conjunction with the granting of a marketing authorization.

Supportive Data

Data on the efficacy and/or safety of an investigational product that were not generated in a pivotal study but that are required as supportive data in a Marketing Authorization Application.

Survival Analysis

A statistical analysis method used, for example, to evaluate the mortality rate in a clinical trial involving a life-threatening medical condition.

SUSAR

Suspected unexpected serious adverse reaction. A SUSAR is an adverse event which qualifies as a serious event as defined by the six criteria under the heading **Serious Adverse Event (SAE) Criteria,** might be related to the study drug, **and is unexpected** when referenced against the Investigator's Brochure and/or the Summary of Product Characteristics.

Technical Complaint

Any indication of the failure of a product to meet customer or user expectation for safety and/or quality. The complaint alleges deficiencies related to safety, quality, identity, purity or potency of a product after it is released for distribution.

Template

A pre-prepared document outline that provides structure and supports uniformity in appearance and formatting of documents of the same type or class. Templates are an important tool to facilitate consistent, efficient and effective creation of important documents.

Test Data

Dummy data used to verify the database set up and structure, and the validation and query resolution processes.

Test Facility

Test facility means the persons, premises and operational unit(s) that are necessary for conducting the non-clinical health and environmental safety study. For multi-site studies, those which are conducted at more than one site, the test facility comprises the site at which the Study Director is located and all individual test sites, which individually or collectively can be considered to be test facilities.

Therapeutic Area/Field

A field of medicine (e.g. gastrointestinal, immunological, cardiovascular).

Tolerability

The ability of a subject to tolerate an investigational product for the duration of the period of treatment.

Trial Master File (TMF)

The TMF is the central receptacle for all the sponsor's essential documents relating to the conduct of the clinical trial (i.e. those documents which individually and collectively permit evaluation of the conduct of a trial and the quality of the data produced); will usually be audited by the sponsor's independent audit function and inspected by the regulatory authority(ies). The TMF consists of a Study Master File, a Country Master File and Site Master Files, as appropriate.

Trial Site

[ICH GCP 1.59] The location(s) where trial-related activities are actually conducted (see also Clinical Trial/Investigational Site).

Trial-Specific Procedure (TSP)

A detailed account of activities to be performed during the conduct of a specific clinical trial. The TSP is a supplement to other project relevant documents such as the clinical trial protocol, SOP or PSP. TSPs are created, maintained and managed by the issuing clinical team.

Type 1 Error

An error that is made when a correct null hypothesis is rejected (false positive).

Type 1 Query

Addresses an issue identified during the review of a clinical trial database (e.g. an omission, inaccuracy or inconsistency) that can be resolved on the basis of data already provided by the investigator in the data record for that trial, site and patient. A type 1 query does not need to be validated by the investigator. The investigator is however informed of the correction undertaken.

Type 2 Error

An error that is made when an incorrect null hypothesis is not rejected (false negative).

Type 2 Query

Addresses an issue identified during the review of a clinical trial database (e.g. an omission, inaccuracy or inconsistency) that cannot be resolved on the basis of data already provided by the investigator in the data record for that trial, site and patient. A type 2 query addresses an issue that can only be resolved in collaboration with the investigator. Resolution of a type 2 query must be validated by the investigators dated signature.

Unexpected Adverse Event/Adverse Drug Reaction

[ICH GCP 1.60] An adverse event/reaction, the nature and severity of which is not consistent with the applicable product information (e.g. Investigator's Brochure for an unapproved investigational product or package insert/Summary of Product Characteristics for an approved product).

Validation

Confirmation, through the provision of objective evidence, that the requirements for a specific intended use or application have been fulfilled.

Variance

The square of the standard deviation.

Verification

A means by which data are checked to confirm their accuracy.

Visual Analog Scale (VAS)

A scale used to provide quantitative measurements of subjective parameters, frequently a 10-cm line with definitions attached to each end (e.g. 'No pain at all'; 'Worst pain ever experienced'). The subject is required to mark the place on the line that he/she believes best represents the severity of his/her symptoms.

Vital Signs

The assessment of systolic and diastolic blood pressure, heart rate, temperature, weight, and/or respiratory rate.

Volunteer

A subject, normally healthy, participating in a Phase 1 study.

Vulnerable Subjects

[ICH GCP 1.61] Individuals whose willingness to volunteer to participate in a clinical trial may be unduly influenced by the expectation, whether justified or not, of benefits associated with participation, or of a retaliatory response from senior members of a hierarchy in case of refusal to participate. Examples are members of a group with a hierarchical structure, such as medical, pharmacy, dental, and nursing students, subordinate hospital and laboratory personnel, employees of the pharmaceutical industry, members of the armed forces, and persons kept in detention. Other vulnerable subjects include patients with incurable diseases, persons in nursing homes, unemployed or impoverished persons, patients in emergency situations, ethnic minority groups, homeless persons, nomads, refugees, minors and those incapable of giving consent.

Washout Period

The period between two active treatments (e.g. previous medication and investigational product; two treatments in a clinical trial) during which time the subject receives no active treatment, except, where permitted, rescue medication unrelated to the investigational product(s) (see also Run-in Period).

Well-Being (of Trial Subjects)

[ICH GCP 1.62] The physical and mental integrity of the subjects participating in a clinical trial.

Withdrawals

Subjects who are withdrawn prematurely from a clinical trial by the investigator. See also Drop Out.

Within Subject/Patient Comparison

Comparison between the effects of two or more treatments in subjects acting as their own control in a cross-over study.

Witnessed Consent

See Impartial Witness.

Health Authority Addresses in the European Area

Austria	Austrian Federal Office for Safety in Health Care	www.basg.at/en/
Belgium	Federal Agency for Medicines and Health Products	www.fagg-afmps.be/en/
Bulgaria	Bulgarian Drug Agency	www.bda.bg
Cyprus	Ministry of Health	www.moh.gov.cy/moh/ moh.nsf/index_en/index_en
Czech Republic	State Institute for Drug Control (SUKL)	www.sukl.cz/index. php?lchan=1&lred=1
Denmark	Danish Medicines Agency	www.dkma.dk
Estonia	State Agency of Medicines	www.ravimiamet.ee
European Union	European Medicines Agency (EMA)	www.ema.europa.eu
Finland	Finnish Medicines Agency	www.fimea.fi
France	Agence Francaise de Securite Sanitaire des Produits de Sante (afssaps)	www.afssaps.fr
Germany	Federal Institute for Drugs and Medical Devices (BfArM)	www.bfarm.de
Greece	National Organization for Medicines	eof1.eof.gr/eof_en/enhome. html
Hungary	National Institute of Pharmacy	www.ogyi.hu/main_page/
Iceland	Icelandic Medicines Agency	www.imca.is/
Ireland	Irish Medicines Board	www.imb.ie
Italy	Italian Medicines Agency (AIFA)	www.agenziafarmaco.it
Latvia	Latvian State Agency of Medicines (ZVA)	www.zva.gov.lv/index.php
Lithuania	Lithuanian State Medicines Control Agency (VVKT)	www.vvkt.lt/index.php
Luxembourg	Ministry for Health	www.ms.public.lu
Malta	Medicines Authority	medicinesauthority.gov.mt

Netherlands	Medicines Evaluation Board	www.cbg-meb.nl/cbg/en
Norway	Norwegian Medicines Agency	www.legemiddelverket.no
Poland	The Office for Registration of Medicinal Products, Medical Devices and Biocidal Products	en.urpl.gov.pl
Portugal	National Authority of Medicines and Health Products	www.infarmed.pt
Romania	Ministry of Health	www.anm.ro/en/home.html
Slovakia	State Institute for Drug Control	www.sukl.sk/en
Slovenia	Agency for Medicinal Products and Medical Devices	www.jazmp.si/index.php?id=56
Spain	Spanish Agency for Medicines and Medical Devices	www.aemps.es/en/home.htm
Sweden	Medical Product Agency	www.lakemedelsverket.se/english/
United Kingdom	Medicines and Healthcare Products Regulatory Agency (MHRA)	www.mhra.gov.uk